Visual Manna's Master Drawing

by
Rich and Sharon Jeffus

This book is dedicated to all of our students that have become a part of our lives.

Copyright 1999
Visual Manna
P.O. Box 553
Salem, Missouri 65560
573-729-2100
573-453-6364
ISBN 0-9677386-2-8

Table of Contents

SKETCH BOOK

This is a daily assignment best geared to the most serious artists. It is also one of the most dramatic ways to improve artistic skills in a short period of time. Have your student keep a sketch book. This should become a constant companion to the student and needs to be a tag-a-long wherever the student goes. As a continual project, have the student sketch five objects each day. These need to be real everyday objects; not something that is in the mind or from a photograph or painting. (The student can draw imaginary things, but they are not included in the assigned five objects). Finding five objects to draw is simple. Have the student look at the normal things around him. An example would be the tissue box on the table, the table itself, the pencil in the hand that is drawing, the wall, the chair, the car keys, the radio, etc. These sketches are just sketches. They are not finished works of art. They need to be done from the viewpoint and the perspective of the artist. The young artist should practice speed, but the main point is to have the sketches represent real objects. Try to draw clocks, shoes, even books. Take a single object and draw it from many different angles. Draw what you see, not what you think you see. Draw the object, rotate it a little and draw it again. Lower the object down or raise it up and draw it again. Stand over the object and draw it as you look straight down. If the object is big enough (like a chair), crawl under it and draw it from underneath. The combinations are endless.

Another good exercise to learn to draw is to take a piece of black construction paper and cut out several odd

Black Paper Cutout

shapes. Next, place some tracing paper beside the cutouts and draw them. DO NOT TRACE. Draw the cutout as best you can. After you get it like you want it, place the tracing paper over the cutout. You can see how close you are. This is good training for hand eye coordination. Draw very lightly at first: so lightly that if someone sits across from you, they could not see the

lines. These lines are only "construction" lines. They are a close representation of the form you want to draw, but they are not the form. After you have lightly drawn the entire shape; stop. Hold the page away from you. Stand up and move away if needed. Turn the page upside down. You may want to hold it up to a mirror, or if the paper is thin, hold it up to the light and look at it from the back. Look at it carefully. What is different from that which you are drawing? After you have closely inspected the lightly drawn picture, make any changes you feel are necessary. Do the close inspection again. If you are doing a major work, it may be good to leave it alone for sometime. Often, after a short time away from my work I can see things in a new, fresh way and can see places I really messed up. After you are quite satisfied the picture is exactly like you want, then start darkening the lines.

Sometimes it is best if you do not erase on your paper. This is especially true if you are using expensive, high quality paper, such as 140 lb. watercolor paper or anytime you are planning to use watercolor or markers on the picture. Paper, comes with many different finishes. Some of these finishes are unable to stand the pressure of erasing. When you erase on certain paper it tears the surface fibers. Where these fibers are torn, the paper takes the color differently. This is particularly true if the color is watery or is a light color such as yellow. If the paper surface has been disturbed, the beautiful yellow sunlight may turn orange when it reaches the torn fibers. To avoid this, draw your preliminary sketches on a separate piece of paper. Transfer the sketch to the good paper. An easy way to do this is to turn your original sketch over, and using a soft pencil, cover the back of the page dark. This makes a graphite paper. Turn the sketch back over and place it on top of your good paper. Draw over the lines of your sketch that you want to keep, and it will press the graphite from the back of your sketch onto the good paper. This leaves a light pencil drawing that can be colored without any torn paper fibers to worry about.

Glossary of Words To Know

Atmosphere Perspective - A way of showing distance in a picture by having muted colors in the background or distance, and darker and brighter colors in the foreground.

Balance - The arrangement of lines and shapes and tones in a picture which give it a visual balance. There are things equally interesting on both sides of the picture.

Contour Line - A contour line is the line around an object or form.

Contrast - The difference between the dark and light areas.

Drawing - A sketch, design or representation usually made on paper with pen, pencil, pastels, charcoal or chalk.

Form - The external shape or appearance of a representation.

Grid - A network of evenly spaced horizontal and vertical lines placed over a picture to assist in realistic drawing of the picture.

Half-tone - The area of a subject that is lighted by a light source between the full light and the shadow or shadow edge.

Horizon Line - The place where the sky and earth seem to come together.

Implied Texture - This is when you draw something that looks like it has texture.

Light Source - This can be the sun, a lamp or a window. Knowing your light source can help you with your drawings.

Overlap - A simple technique that shows perspective. One object is placed in front of another. A good example would be a parade scene where you see uniforms up close and in the distance the uniforms resting on top of another. Overlapping can make things look closer of further away. It is also effective in creating a visual rhythm.

Perspective - One point perspective is sometimes called a linear perspective. It is defined as a mathematical system of representing a three dimensional reality in only two dimensions. A one point has all lines converging into one vanishing point. A two point perspective also represents mathematically three dimensional space on a two dimensional surface, but has two separate vanishing points.

Rhythm - A regular repetition of line of forms that can denote motion.

Scale - The relative size of objects in a picture. How large or small objects appear next to each other.

Shading - The use of different values in dark and light on an object to make it look realistic. Shading shows the shadow and the light in a picture. It gives roundness to otherwise flat parts of your drawing. When you draw, if you apply more pressure on your pencil, the shading will be darker.

Still Life - A representation of inanimate objects.

Texture - Texture is how something feels.

Value - In art, this is the shades (degrees) of darkness or lightness.

Vanishing Point - The point at which something disappears into the horizon. The point where parallel lines appear to meet and disappear. When we stand and look down railroad tracks that are straight, they appear to meet at a single point.

4

INTRODUCTION

Drawing is a learned skill. It is the same as sewing or playing the piano. There are some people naturally talented in sewing, piano and drawing, but nobody, to my knowledge, was ever born knowing all there is to know about sewing, piano or drawing.

Sometimes these skills come easy. It often seems easy to the person that loves what they are doing. This, however, is not always the case. There are times when someone will really love piano, sewing or art, but will have a very difficult time getting it right. Sometimes, they practice and practice and feel they will never be able to do it. The works they attempt seem too complex and unattainable. The practice is often boring. Then one day, almost undetected by themselves, the things they do become simple, easy, and they start creating works beyond their wildest expectations.

When you are in the middle of the practice, don't get discouraged. If you want to become good at what you are doing you must practice. It is easy to be discouraged. When you practice and work hard, sometimes you see someone who never seems to try and does it well. You may tell yourself, "What is the use to go on; I will never be that good?" Yes, they may have a gift. Yes, it is hard for you. But your desire to be a great artist is in you, not by chance. Maybe not even by choice. It is there given by God. A deep held conviction is conformation that what you want to be is from God. It may be that what God wants to communicate through art can only be done through you. He may want to use you, your personality and your life experiences to demonstrate who He is to others.

In the Bible, in Exodus Chapter 31 God says something curious.

Exodus 31:1 ¶ And the LORD spake unto Moses, saying, 2 See, **I have called by name Bezaleel** the son of Uri, the son of Hur, of the tribe of Judah: 3 And **I have filled him with the spirit of God, in wisdom, and in understanding, and in knowledge, and in all manner of workmanship,** 4 To devise cunning works, to work in gold, and in silver, and in brass, 5 And in cutting of stones, to set them, and in carving of timber, to work in all manner of workmanship.

Isn't that interesting? When you think of someone being called by name, you think of being called to be a preacher, called to be a missionary or called to be a doctor. There, in Exodus, the man Bezaleel was called to be an artist! To do beautiful art work for the tabernacle of God!

The purpose of this book is to help students with their drawing skill. I always try to teach the drawing basics, and within this framework allow each student as much freedom as possible to develop their own style. I found students enjoyed their work and did a better job if I allowed them to choose a subject they had a feeling for. Some students love western art; some prefer landscape and nature study; athletic art (pictures of athletes in action) is also popular. Once the drawing basics are taught, much freedom needs to be given in the choice of a topic. Each student of drawing has a distinct and individual style that needs to be developed. This is one reason to expose students to many different artists and styles. I even had one college painting teacher who instructed us to do ten copies of the masters in painting, before we first attempted our own.

Many professional artists do preliminary sketching and photographing of what they want to draw or paint before they begin.

For a free drawing board, go to your local hardware store and ask them for their discontinued masonite samples.

5

I believe it is important to see how a real professional artist draws. David Plank, one of the most outstanding bird artists in America, has graciously allowed us to look at some of his preliminary sketches and studies of various birds. You can see some of David's field drawings on pages 73-75 of this book. He has definitely developed a distinctive style in his drawings and paintings of birds. David Plank has had eleven cover paintings for the magazine *The Bird Watcher's Digest*. He has been accepted in numerous national and international art shows and won several awards. He has approximately 1200 water color paintings and 50,000 field drawings of birds to his credit.

More than this, he is a tremendous encouragement to children and young people in their appreciation of birds. He takes part in various community and school activities and takes every opportunity to encourage young people to study and be involved in art and especially birds. Perhaps you have an artist in your community who will allow your students or children to visit their studio. It will be an enriching time for your young artists. David Plank communicates to us his love for and appreciation of birds. Can you think of something you want to communicate visually? Are you willing to practice...practice...practice...to succeed?

A PHILOSOPHY OF ART
by
David Plank

Whether we plan to pursue a career as an artist or not, an introduction to art and the process of drawing and painting will enrich our lives and give us a greater awareness of the world around us.

If we do become artists, what we create should not only be meaningful for us, but affect others in a positive way.

Everyone, regardless of economic or ethnic background, has an obligation to do what they can to improve society. As artists, we have a unique opportunity in this respect. We have the possibility of creating art which can bring light to the eyes of those viewing it. Indeed, life without art is less civilized.

Although the mechanical side of creating art---the act of drawing and painting---requires a great deal of work and practice in order to be skilled, the creation of art is more about a way of seeing and thinking. The word "create" tells us that art is not about copying what we see, but expressing our thoughts and feelings; thereby "creating" something new and original.

The physical subject matter of a painting can be quite secondary to the real message of the painting. In my case, birds have always been meaningful for me and the inspiration for creating art through which I can express myself and communicate some of those thoughts and feelings to others.

For more than fifty years I have sketched birds in fields and forests; using these drawings, and the experience of being outdoors, to create watercolor paintings. While art is the purpose of these paintings, I hope they also will influence people to care more about birds and the natural world which is required for their survival, as well as our own. Some may be inspired to become bird watchers; one of the most civilized activities of mankind.

To contact David Plank concerning his wonderful prints of birds write:
David Plank
P.O. Box 751
Salem, Missouri, 65560.

The Visual Manna philosophy of art is this. Art is more than just being able to draw. Art is more than being able to paint or do sculptures. Art is being creative. God is creative. Have you ever seen a duck billed platypus? God has created us in His image. Part of that image is His creative nature.

Sometimes children can get frustrated when doing art. This is often, in part, a problem that their brains (creative nature) are lagging behind their technology or physical development. Technology problems occur when the child has ideas best rendered in pen and ink and they only know crayons. Or the idea is in tempera paint, and could best be demonstrated with computer cinematography. Physical development or fine motor skill development or manual dexterity develops at different rates depending on the child. Because this will improve as the child ages and practices, it is of little importance in teaching art. Probably the most important thing is to let the children create and to encourage them.

How do you hold the pencil?

Some say to hold the pencil between the tips of all of the fingers of the hand. Some say to hold it like you do when you write. Some hold the pencil by the sides and place the index finger on the pencil lead point. I say that you should hold your pencil in any way you are comfortable. You are in charge of the pencil, not the other way around. I will often use all of the above techniques along with others on any picture depending on the results I want to accomplish. Holding the pencil closer to the point makes it easier to make a dark line, and if you hold the point sideways, you can make a thicker line.

Let's talk about supplies.

Lets talk about paper and pencils. Paper comes in pound weight and texture. To understand the weight of paper you must first understand that a real sheet of paper is 17 inches wide and 22 inches long. What we see in "regular" typing is a sheet cut into four pieces. This makes them 8 1/2 inches by 11 inches. Regular typing paper is called 20 pound paper. This means if you had 1000 whole sheets of paper they would weigh 20 pounds. Typing paper also has a smooth finish. The finish on paper is called the tooth. Twenty pound smooth tooth paper is good for typing or copy machines, but not for drawing. Good drawing paper should be at least 60 pound and should have a fine tooth. The fine tooth is hard to describe, but once you feel it next to typing paper, you will know. It feels rough, but not coarse.

Pencils do not have any lead in them anymore.

The Egyptians ruled lines with metallic lead, as did medieval monks. The earliest pencils were charcoal or lumps of colored earth or chalk. The so-called lead pencil—a rod of graphite encased in wood—came into use in the 16th century. From the late 18th century pulverized graphite was mixed with clay to bind it and to provide different degrees of hardness—the more clay, the

BY RICH & SHARON JEFFUS

harder the pencil. Today, the mixture is forced through dies, cut to the required length, and kiln-fired. The rods are laid in grooves of a thin board; a similar board is placed over them, and the wood is shaped into pencils, usually of round or hexagonal cross section.

7

All of this about pencils is important because when you start sketching, it is important to draw lightly. If you cannot make a sketch that is so light that it cannot be seen from five feet away, you may need to get a harder pencil. Use a 5H or 6H, but experiment to find what works best for you. Now some of you are ready for and are comfortable with using B or soft pencils. Maybe you like the dramatic look. This is okay if you are confident of your line and never have to erase. For the rest of us, a light touch or hard pencil is best.

Now a word about three dimensions.
IN SCIENCE

In science, the universe can be said to exist as a trinity. That being the trinity of time, space and matter. Each of these is in itself a trinity.

Time comes in past, present and future.
Matter comes in solids, liquids and gases.
Space is anything that occupies three dimensions --and it could be said that space comes in: height, width and length.

The present time you are in is no different than the past time you just left and no different than the future time you are going into. It is your relationship to it that makes it seem different. But there is only one time.

Liquid water is really the same matter as solid water (ice), which is the same material as gaseous water, (steam.) It is your relationship to it that makes it seem different. But there is only one matter.

An object that occupies a space has a height, width and a length, but is only one object. Hold an object in your hand. Look at it from only one side and see its width. Next, look at it from one

side as to view its length. Next view it from an end where you can only see its height. There is only one object in your hand. It is your relationship to the object that gives you three distinct sides to observe. Maybe God is something like the things He has created. Like time, space and matter, God may be a trinity that reveals different sides of Himself to each of us depending on your relationship to Him or His relationship to you.

God said in Romans 1:20, "For the invisible things of him from the creation of the world are clearly seen, being understood by the things that are made, even

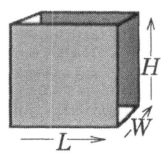

his eternal power and Godhead; so that they are without excuse:" This means that you can know something about God by looking at what He has created.

Making Something Three Dimensional
IN ART

In art, there are also three dimensions. To end some confusion, art is divided into three separate categories. One dimensional art is anything flat. Paintings, pencil drawings, charcoal, watercolor etc. are all one dimensional art. Two dimensional art is anything carved into a surface or raised off of a surface. Three dimensional art is sculpture or statues, or anything you walk all the way around and it still looks like something. Clothes, cereal boxes, drink cans and cars are all examples of three dimensional art. Artist touch many more things than you might have imagined.

8

LESSON 1

Shading a cylinder or a sphere.

The quickest way to make something look three dimensional is to apply, shading, shadow and texture.

The purpose of shading is to make the object dark on one side and light on the other, with the easiest gradient as possible.

LIGHT

Draw a cylinder.

Pick the direction the light is coming from.

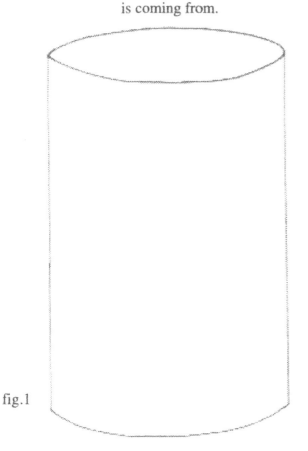

fig.1

the shade. #3 is just straight lines, the more lines the darker. #4 is contour lines. These lines follow the shape. The lines are made longest first, and then shorter and shorter lines are added between each line. #5 is shading made by a pile of pencil lead (graphite) placed on the paper and spread out with a smudge stick or forefinger.

LIGHT

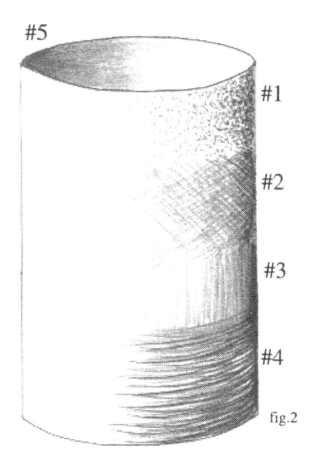

fig.2

Shade the cylinder. Try several techniques to determine which one you like best. Some techniques may work better for you on one kind of picture than another, so get familiar with all of them.

In fig.2, I used several techniques on the same cylinder. #1 is pointillism; the use of dots or points; the more dots, the darker the shading. #2 is cross hatching, the more cross hatch the darker

A large part of being an artist is being observant. Take your drawings and really look at them. Turn them upside down and look carefully. Turn them over on the back and look through the paper, by holding it up to a light. What do you see? Are all the vertical lines really vertical. Get a straight edge and lay it a long a supposed straight line, is it straight? Next time as you begin drawing, remember what you observed and make corrections before you darken your lines.

9

This sphere, fig.1, was shaded with a combination of techniques. Draw several basic shapes and shade them in using various techniques. Try doing cones, cylinders, rods and spheres.

fig.1

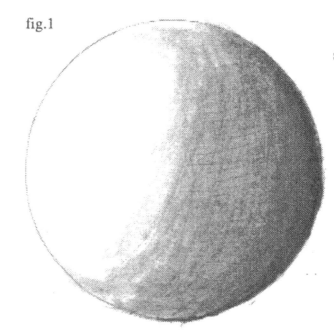

This is an example of a sphere shaded with a single light source.

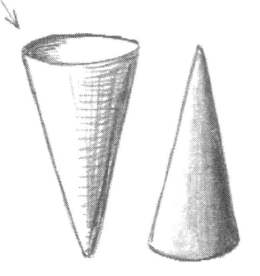

Cones

So far we have been doing objects with curved surfaces.

Notice this example of incorrect shading below. The cube's sides look rounded. This is because the use of a gradient makes the flat sides curve. I would not say, "Never shade like this." Someday you may want a metallic look. Which is what the cube below looks like. But in general, to make a cube look "right", keep each side flat by the use of uniform shading as explained earlier.

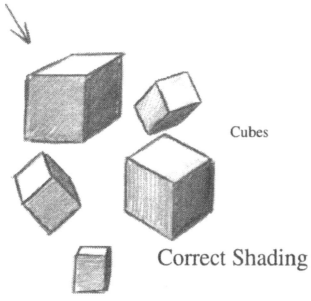

Cubes

Correct Shading

When you shade things with flat sides such as cubes, you shade each side the same tone, like the ones above. This is because the side is not curved. Each side should have a slightly different shade, depending on the light source.

Incorrect Shading

As part of this lesson find some real objects that represent basic shapes. Cylinder shapes for example are hair spray cans, flashlight batteries, soup cans, paper towel rolls, bananas, carrots or telescopes. Sphere shapes are, marbles, balls, green peas, frog eggs, oranges or apples. Get several examples and draw them from different angles. Be careful to draw what you see, not what you think you see. A good artist is a good observer.

10

Shade each object as you see it. If it does not have a definite light source, move it to a light source. For the time being, don't try to imagine the shading, set it up so that it has shading.

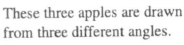
These three apples are drawn from three different angles.

Remember to draw what you see, not what you think you see.

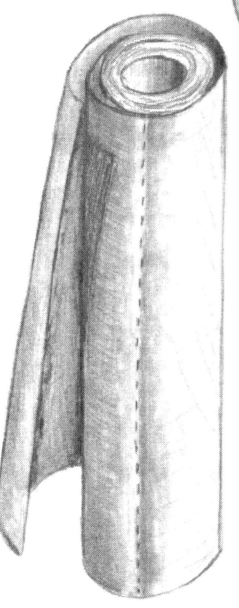

Remember this is an exercise in shading. And you need to draw from **REAL** objects, not from any pictures. Not even from these great examples! There will be an opportunity in the next lesson to use your imagination.

Artists have always drawn from real things. Until the 1830's, there were no photographs to draw from. When Leonardo da Vinci painted the Mona Lisa, he had her sitting in front of him. He did not dream up her smile!

Nearly Empty Paper Towel Roll

11

These plates came from my sketch book. They are a study in foreshortening. Foreshortening is the apparent change of shape as an object as it is tilted or receding from or projected away from the viewer. An example of this is when someone is pointing directly at you or away from you. If someone is pointing their finger at you, all you can see is the tip of the finger, some knuckles and some roundness of the forearm. Another example is a ceiling fan. If you are right under it when it is spinning fast, what you see are the blade tips as they inscribe a circle in space. If you were standing on a ladder at eye level with the moving fan blades, you would see a line. The shape the spinning blades inscribe in space has to change from a line to a perfect circle. It goes through a series of squashed circles called ellipses. That is foreshortening. That is also what these plates are doing. If you are looking straight at the plate's edge, it is almost a line. The farther you move the plate up or down, the more like a circle it becomes.

I want to mention your sketch books again. Almost every drawing in this book was at one time part of my sketch book. All of my paintings, charcoal, pencil and ink drawings all have their roots in some sketch book. Drawing everyday objects may seem boring sometimes, but the practice you gain from doing them can not be over emphasized. If you do get bored, start putting the pictures together in imaginative ways. Draw your car, but have it on the living room chair. Draw a spoon with a tree in it. The combinations are endless. The most important things are to draw real things. Draw them like you see them and not how you think you see them. And as you draw remember: shape (outline), shadow, shading and texture.

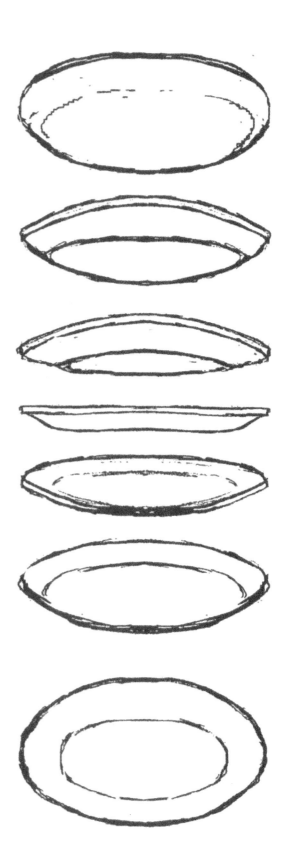

LESSON 2

Creativity

In this lesson we want to be creative. Draw something never before seen by mankind. It can be animal, vegetable or mineral. I find it best to draw animals, but that is only my preference.

First, do an outline picture. You may want to lay-out the picture using circles or basic shapes to "hold the space" until you get the whole picture.

Second, determine which direction the light is coming from.

Third, start shading your picture, as if each individual part was a cylinder, cone, sphere or cube.

Next, give your creation shadows. Shadows generally fall directly in line with the direction the light is going, and roughly approximate the shape of the object that is casting the shadow.

Give your picture texture. If you did an animal, you can do fir, feathers, or scales.

fig.1

Cylinder casting a shadow.

Scale your picture by putting something of known size in your picture. In (fig. 1) the picture is scaled with the finger the critter is standing on.

If I would have drawn a skyscraper in this picture as big as the critter's toe, it would make it seem much larger.

The picture has several other features you can put in a drawing to make it better. Center of interest should be the place your eye first goes in a picture. Some artists, when using color, will put a little red on the center of interest to catch the eye.

LIGHT DIRECTION

This picture also has depth. It is illustrated by the trees in the distance being smaller than the trees in the foreground. The last two things this picture has are the name of the artist and date. Artist have two ways that they use to sign their work. One way is to sign it along the edge or around the border. If you do this, make sure it is far enough from the edge that a frame would not cover it up. The other way to sign a picture is to make it part of the picture. In the picture above, it is signed along the edge of the finger and on the critter's bracelet as examples.

13

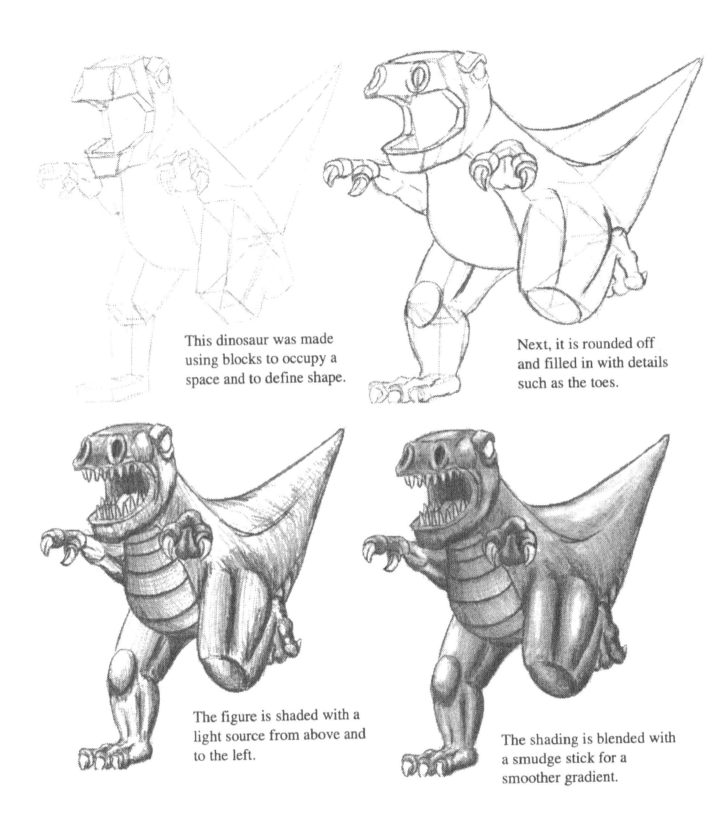

This dinosaur was made using blocks to occupy a space and to define shape.

Next, it is rounded off and filled in with details such as the toes.

The figure is shaded with a light source from above and to the left.

The shading is blended with a smudge stick for a smoother gradient.

14

Scales are added for texture. To finish this picture it would need; shadows, and perhaps something to scale the picture, props, a consideration of center of interest, and establishing depth within the picture, and of course, the artist's name and the date.

15

Here are a several more examples of everyday sketches from my sketch book. One is a dented "Roasted Garlic and Onion" Spaghetti can, another is a book on a coffee table, and the last is an old toothbrush. Each started out as a basic shape. The can is a cylinder. The toothbrush and book are rectangles. The can might tell an interesting story if it was by my backpack or camp fire.

LESSON 3

Really Seeing

The previous lessons used a lot of imagination. For the most part creativity is good, and to have a great imagination is essential to being a good artist, but it is also important to be able to draw from reality. When Raphael wanted to draw a dragon, (dinosaur), he first learned all he could about his subject from eyewitness accounts, then he looked at reptiles he had available such as snakes and lizards and combined them with bat wings and other animal parts to produce a life like animal for his picture "St. George and the Dragon." When Steven Spielberg wanted to create lifelike dinosaurs for his movie "Jurassic Park," he first studied large animals such as rhinos, elephants and giraffes to see how they moved and how the skin flexed. He then copied what he found. To start drawing from reality sometimes is difficult. This is particularly true if you have only drawn from your imagination or copied other pictures.

Something that is handy, (so to speak), to draw from real life is your own hand. This is not easy. But the way to get better is to practice, practice, practice.

When you draw your hand, if you straighten out your fingers, it will be easier; if you bend your fingers it will be a little harder. Stretch yourself if you can; that is the only way you can grow. If you are younger, if you want to trace your hand, it will be okay. If you do trace your hand, the main point of the lesson is to shade your fingers as if they are cylinders.

Remember to pick a light source so as to give the hand shadows and shade.

Again, draw what you see! Many young people tend to draw their fingernails like this.

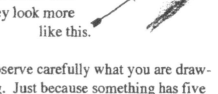

If you observe carefully, you will notice that they look more like this.

Observe carefully what you are drawing. Just because something has five lobes on it, it doesn't make it a hand. The difference is in the details!

Many times children have a difficult time drawing things as complicated as a hand because they try to draw the picture as a whole, using a continuous contour line. They generally start drawing from

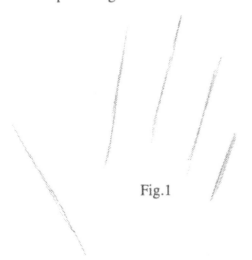

the thumb and continue to the little finger without hardly picking up their pencils. This method can work if you have good coordination between the pencil and your eyes.

For the person wanting to learn to draw, it is a better idea to break the object up into smaller pieces and do one section at a time. Another way to look at it is that you can establish mid point corrections, so you will end up where you want to go. Much like astronauts do when trying to get to the moon and back. If you don't hit the midpoint you will miss the last point. Fig.1

Fig.1

Look at you hand and pretend that it has lines that run down the middle of your fingers. Draw these lines on a piece of paper. They should look something like the one above.

Next, lay a pencil across your finger tips. Fig.2 Look at the angle the pencil makes and place a mark at the same place along the line that repre-

sents the center line of that finger. Do the same with all of the fingers. It should look like Fig.3.

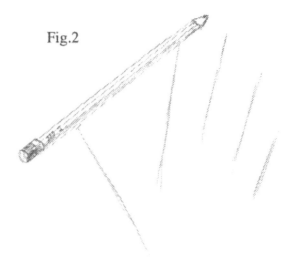

Fig.2

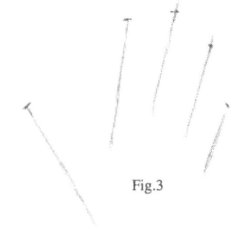

Now that you have all of these points and construction lines, you can add points that represent the valleys between each finger.

Fig.3

After you have all of the "mid-points," now start drawing the hand like you would normally.

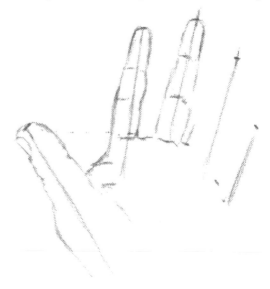

18

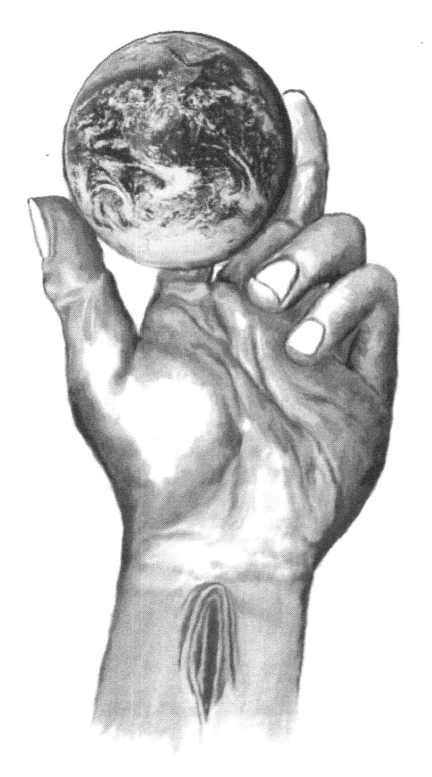

This is an example of drawing from real objects. I used common things in an imaginative way. The hand is mine. It was easy to use. The picture was easy to find. This picture of the world is one of the most widely produced photographs in the history of civilization. It was taken from Apollo 17 and is called the "Blue Marble." If you look around and are observant, you can see it everywhere. The hand has a nail wound in its wrist. It is supposed to be Jesus's hand. The Bible clearly states that Jesus was nailed in His hand. Why would I put the wound in His wrist? There have been studies made over hundreds of years by many scholars trying to determine if someone could be held on a cross with a nail in the hand. They also wanted to know if a body could be held without tearing out through the hand and, would it possible to nail through the hand without breaking any bones? (The Bible said that none of His bones would be broken). The answer to these questions was found in linguistics, not in anatomy. It turns out that the Greek word for "hand," starts at the elbow and goes all the way to the fingertips. The writer of the Greek New Testament didn't have our word for wrist, so he said that Jesus was nailed through His hands.

LESSON 4
Grids

In the same manner that you broke up the drawing of your hand into smaller pieces using construction lines made up of center lines and end points, there is a more formal way of dividing a picture called a grid.

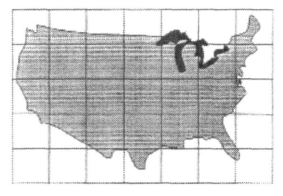

U.S.A. map with grid.

How to Use a Grid

The grid is the easiest way to copy one dimensional art. It is so easy that some people believe that it is almost like cheating. It isn't cheating; many great artists have used grids to transfer their sketches to their canvases. The grid only works on one dimensional art. You will have a hard time drawing grid lines on a statue. There are two ways to use a grid. One way is to do the entire outline first, and then go back and complete the inside. The other way is to do one single square at a time, completing each one before going on to the next. Whichever way you use, try to remember to draw what you see, and not what you think you see. Doing a grid can help you become a better artist by letting you see the relationship between each separate part of a whole drawing. Remember that using a grid is only one way of several in which an artist uses to copy a picture. Some of the other ways will be described later in this book.

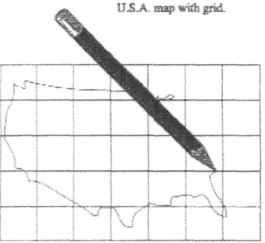

Outline of map being reproduced by carefully drawing line over same grid points.

When you do a grid, the important thing is to observe the relationships between lines or parts of objects in the picture. In the map picture above, you should notice that the tip of Florida is just over the line that runs through the center of the east coast. This is the same thing you were doing with your hand in the previous lesson. When you laid a pencil across the tips of your fingers, you were establishing a relationship between the fingers and illustrated by the angle the pencil made.

Doing grids has some disadvantages. The biggest is that it only works with one dimensional art. This means you are copying flat pictures. The grid does has some clear advantages. The biggest of these is that it is a fast, accurate, and easy way to copy a picture. It helps me most when, after doing many sketches of "real" three dimensional objects in my sketch book, and finally getting the right combination so that it looks just right, I can grid the sketch and get it to my canvas rather quickly, and it will look just like the sketch. Another advantage is that you can, by changing the sizes of the grid lines spacing, make your final work bigger or smaller. If I grid the sketch book with one inch grids, and the canvas with four inch grids, it will be four times as big when completed.

20

Here is an example of doing the grid as a complete line drawing first, and then filling in the details. It is a good idea to count the blocks, to get the placement on the page that you want. I sometimes will number the grid blocks on the picture and then number them the same on the grid paper. This will help keep it straight and keep you from loosing your place.

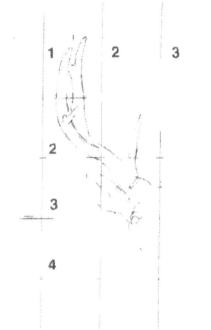

The complete outline is finished and ready to be shaded.

The shading complete and ready to smudge.

21

On this page I used the same picture and the same grid.

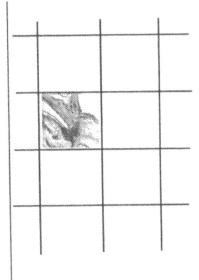

I used a sheet of paper with a hole the size of the grid square to cover all of the picture with the exception of one square. I then drew that one grid square in its entirety (detail lines and shading) before moving on to the next square.

In this picture I used a combination of doing one square at a time and a contour line. This was done so that I could get an idea of how the picture would look when completed.

Find several pictures that you would like to draw. Grid them with one inch squares. Grid your drawing book with the same grid. Try to do the grids in the ways described above. Now do the same picture again, only this time grid your drawing book with two inch grids. Do the picture one more time, only this time grid your drawing with half inch grids. Try to do other pictures. Vary the size of the grid on the picture you are copying. You should notice that close grid lines provide greater detail, but wider lines get done faster.

This is the completed sketch, it has been smudged for a better shade gradient and the hair stroked on for texture. Now it will need the grid lines erased.

22

Now for a practical use of the grid. I choose to explain how to use an invisible grid on this skeleton for two reasons. One, you need to understand the human skeleton to better understand how to draw people. And two, I thought it looked cool!

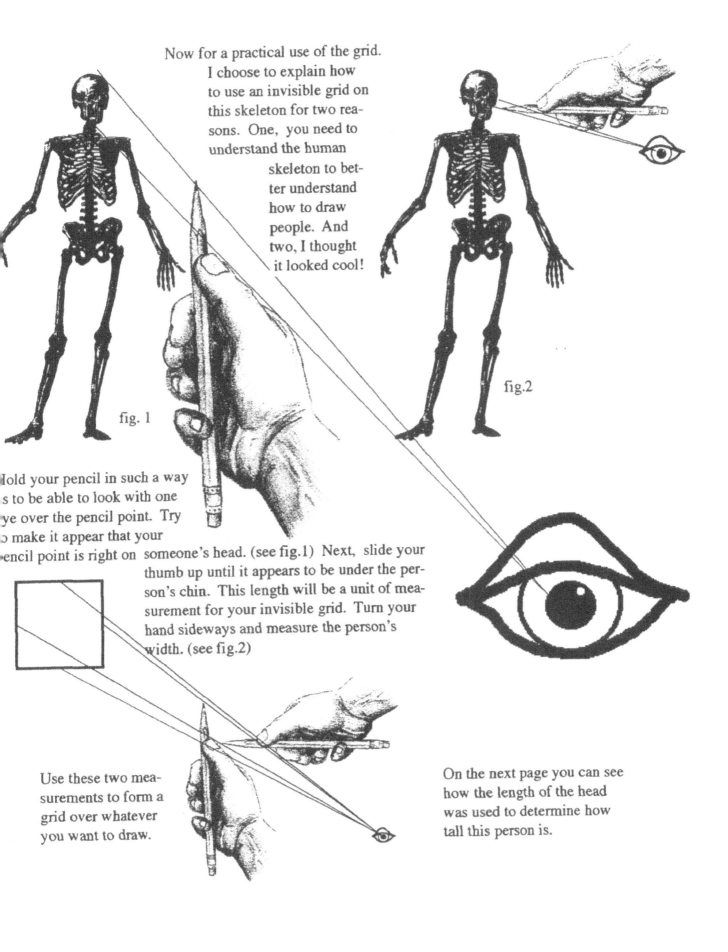

fig. 1

fig.2

Hold your pencil in such a way as to be able to look with one eye over the pencil point. Try to make it appear that your pencil point is right on someone's head. (see fig.1) Next, slide your thumb up until it appears to be under the person's chin. This length will be a unit of measurement for your invisible grid. Turn your hand sideways and measure the person's width. (see fig.2)

Use these two measurements to form a grid over whatever you want to draw.

On the next page you can see how the length of the head was used to determine how tall this person is.

23

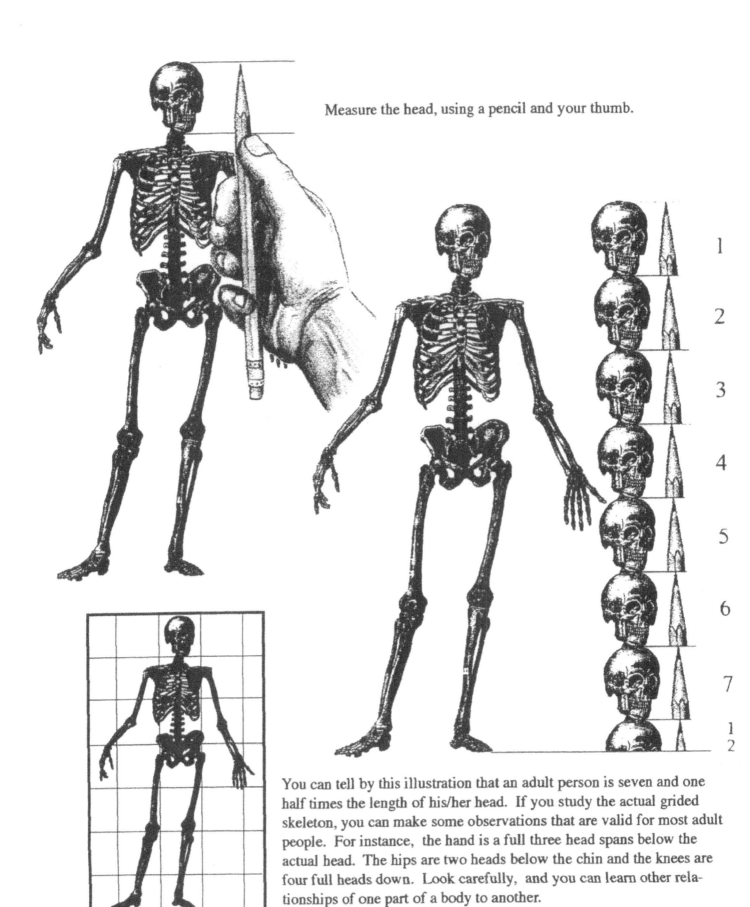

Measure the head, using a pencil and your thumb.

1
2
3
4
5
6
7
1/2

You can tell by this illustration that an adult person is seven and one half times the length of his/her head. If you study the actual grided skeleton, you can make some observations that are valid for most adult people. For instance, the hand is a full three head spans below the actual head. The hips are two heads below the chin and the knees are four full heads down. Look carefully, and you can learn other relationships of one part of a body to another.

24

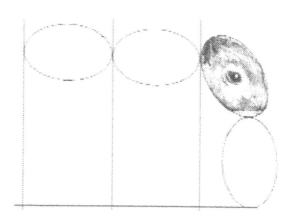

As you can see, I used the head of the squirrel as the unit of measure. This squirrel is roughly three times its head long and two times its head tall. Once I had the head drawn, it was easy to measure the entire squirrel. I used the head to make an invisible grid to draw the rest of the squirrel. If I would have drawn the head four inches long, the finished picture would be approximately twelve inches long and eight inches tall. If I had drawn the head only two inches long the finished picture would be six inches long and four inches tall. After I had the size of the squirrel marked out, I then started doing a contour line drawing. After I had the outline, I shaded the squirrel as if were three dimensional. And lastly, I stroked the hair on to give it texture.

25

LESSON 5

Lets do perspective.

This perspective stuff can be one of the hardest things to learn! It can also be one of the most rewarding. Younger children need to be exposed to this, but they probably won't get it. There is a part of the brain that develops the ability to do logic, algebra and other spatial concepts such as perspective when the child is between 10 to 18 years old. Some children develop this ability earlier and some never do. I tell my students that it took the human race over 5000 years to figure this out and if they don't get it right away, don't worry about it. If the student doesn't understand perspective this time, he or she will have an easier time understanding the next time they try.

Mankind has placed things in the foreground larger and things in the background smaller for centuries. But it wasn't until the middle of the Renaissance that Brunellechi figured out how to do perspective systematically.

To make this as simple as possible, I will introduce two point perspective first and one point last.
They get their names from the number of vanishing points the picture has. However, in reality all pictures are two point perspectives. In a one point, the second point is so far to either the right or left that when lines are drawn to them, the lines appear to be parallel.

I will explain the terminology first. The vanishing point is an infinite point in the distance where all horizontal lines appear to originate. These two points represent the eye level of the viewer of the picture and a line drawn between these points makes the horizon line.

Notice on the two boxes (fig.1), the one above

the horizon line you can see in the bottom and the one below you can see in the top.
Instead of the regular infinite point in the distant, I have replaced them with these eyes.

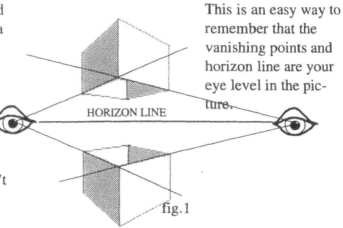

This is an easy way to remember that the vanishing points and horizon line are your eye level in the picture.

HORIZON LINE

fig.1

Look at the desk in front of you. It is below your eyes so you see on top of it.
Now try to see on top of the book case or kitchen cabinets or any other thing that is above your eye level. This same effect takes place in every picture.

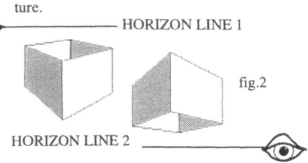

HORIZON LINE 1

fig.2

HORIZON LINE 2

Notice that every picture should have only one set of vanishing points and horizon line. Notice how these boxes (fig.2) look when they are placed side by side, giving the picture two sets of vanishing points.

Thus, it makes the picture look bent, or just out of

26

Let's make a simple box on the horizon line. Because it is right on the line, you cannot see the top of the box or the bottom. Remember to draw these lines very lightly. They are only construction lines and will need to be erased when the box is completed.

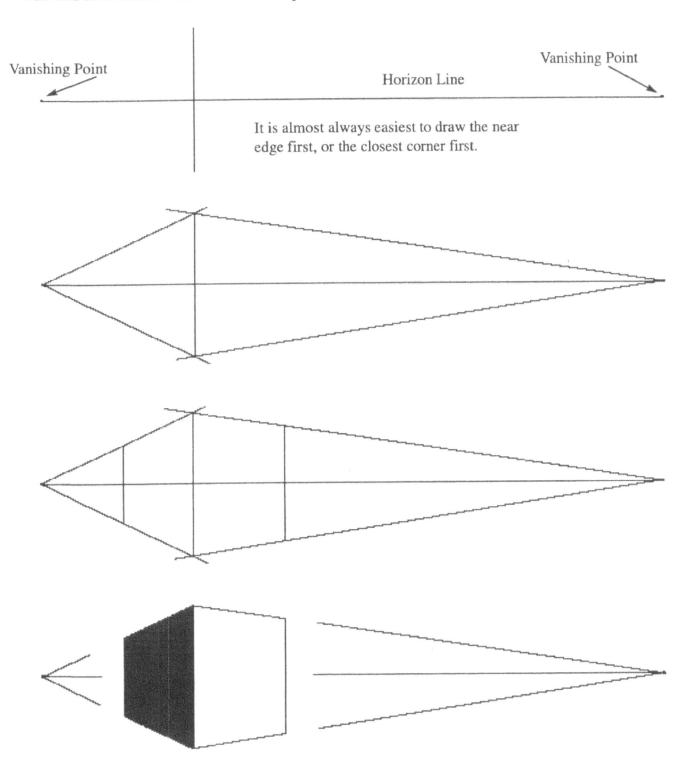

Vanishing Point

Horizon Line

Vanishing Point

It is almost always easiest to draw the near edge first, or the closest corner first.

27

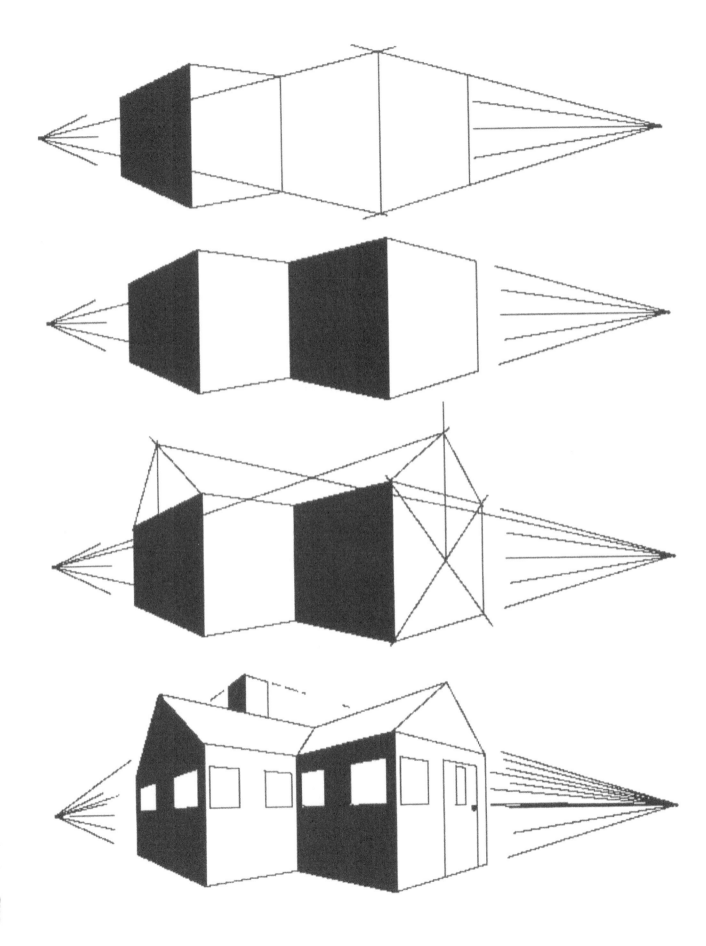

28

One thing you might notice is that the farther the two vanishing points are apart, the more natural the picture looks. Sometimes when doing drawings from photographs, I will find the natural perspective points by placing a straight edge along the roof and foundation lines to see where they come together. This will often be several feet off of the photograph. When I start the drawing, I will tape my paper down in the middle of a table. I then mark the vanishing points on the table. Sometimes, I will tape a string to these places on the table and use the string as a straight edge to draw the right lines.

Sometimes to get a more dramatic look, I will intentionally pull the vanishing points closer together. You have to be careful because if you get the vanishing points too close together, it will make the picture look odd. It will be technically correct, but will not look right.

Below is a box drawn correctly, but as you can see when the vanishing points are put too close together, it begins to look strange. Sometimes I use this radical look to enhance the picture and make it more dramatic. Look at the picture on the next page; it is an example of close vanishing points used to make a more interesting picture.

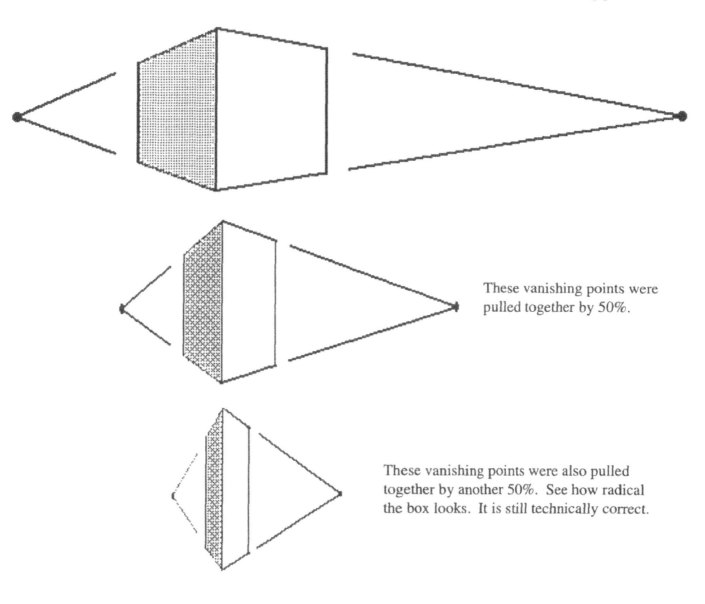

These vanishing points were pulled together by 50%.

These vanishing points were also pulled together by another 50%. See how radical the box looks. It is still technically correct.

In this picture the artist has brought the vanishing points inward. This has exaggerated the perspective. It gives the picture a more dramatic look. The picture, incidentally, was created by placing together three separate sketches in an imaginative way. The trash was from a picture I sketched of a trash heap I found one day as I drove down a long dusty back road in a midwestern state. The chair and the person was someone I placed in the chair and posed to get the proper alignment of the arm and hands to make it more realistic. The TV was one I owned at the time that I copied using perspective.

Of course, you can guess the meaning of the picture. If you watch TV enough, sooner or later it will throw up a load of trash on you!

Jonathan Jeffus (order #332044)

Using this covered bridge as an example of two point perspective drawing, you can see the construction lines used to establish the framework of the bridge.

The end of the bridge is represented by a trapezoid. This is because the things in the foreground are larger than things in the background. You cannot just measure the width of a trapezoid and divide in half to find the center. But it still is easy (see below).

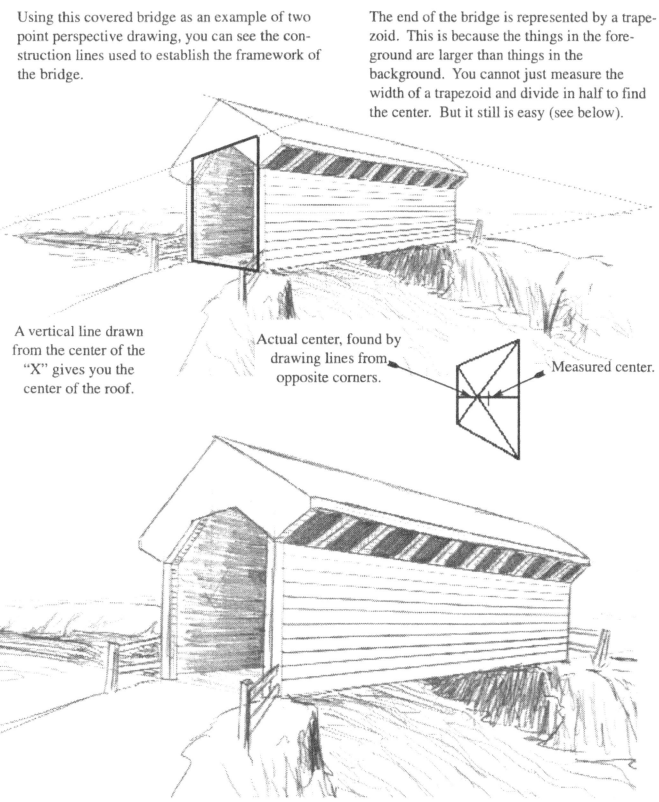

A vertical line drawn from the center of the "X" gives you the center of the roof.

Actual center, found by drawing lines from opposite corners.

Measured center.

To complete this picture will take a realistic background; a background lighter in the distance and darker and clearer towards the foreground.

A prop is something used to help tell a story. This picture could use a horse and carriage or a boy fishing to make it tell a different story.

Drawing a box below the horizontal line is easy. It does have a couple of extra steps because you can see the back edge. Follow the directions below to do a simple box.

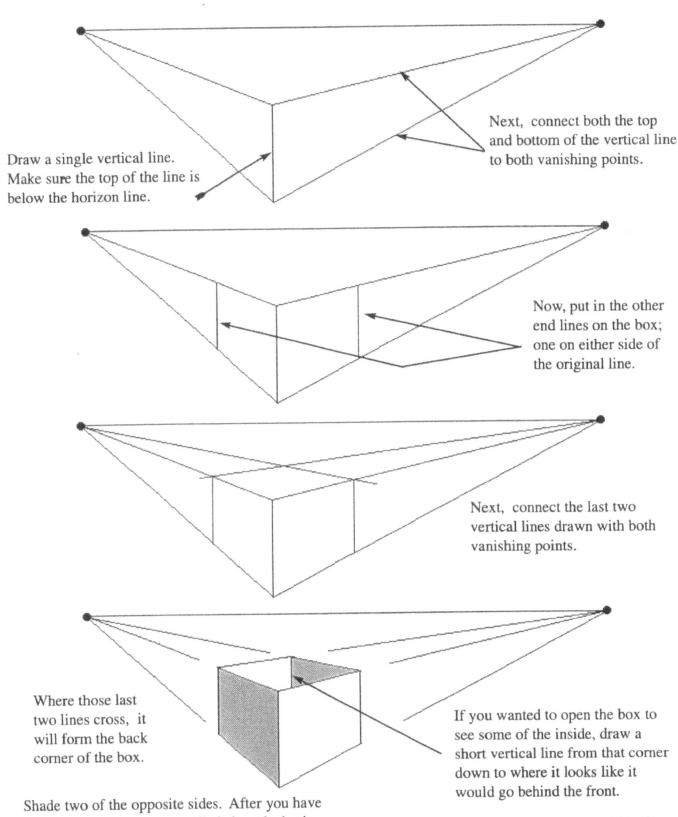

Next, connect both the top and bottom of the vertical line to both vanishing points.

Draw a single vertical line. Make sure the top of the line is below the horizon line.

Now, put in the other end lines on the box; one on either side of the original line.

Next, connect the last two vertical lines drawn with both vanishing points.

Where those last two lines cross, it will form the back corner of the box.

If you wanted to open the box to see some of the inside, draw a short vertical line from that corner down to where it looks like it would go behind the front.

Shade two of the opposite sides. After you have the ability to draw a box easily below the horizon line, try to draw one above the line. You should be able to see under or into the bottom of the box.

If you would like to see what a box would look like drawn above the horizon line, just turn the book over!

32

For the last page of perspective, I have a rare three point perspective. I said rare because for everyday drawing, it is seldom or never used. It is fun to experiment with, and helps the advanced students better understand perspective. I have used this technique for pictures where you want to exaggerate height. I once did a "Tower of Babel" that looked rather dramatic using a three point perspective.

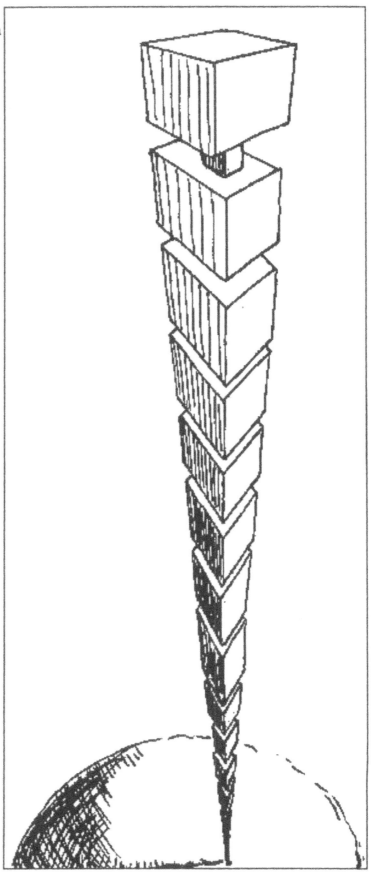

One point perspective can be simple or amazingly difficult. We will start with the simple ones. Remember that technically all pictures are two point perspectives, only sometimes the second vanishing point is so far off the page that any line you draw to it appears to be parallel.

In fig.1, I have placed a horizon line, a vanishing point and three boxes.

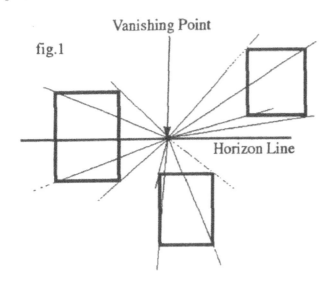

fig.1

Vanishing Point

Horizon Line

The boxes represent the near end of three, three dimensional cubes. One is on the horizon line, one below the horizon line and one above. Fig.2 shows the lines drawn to the vanishing point from the four corners of the boxes.

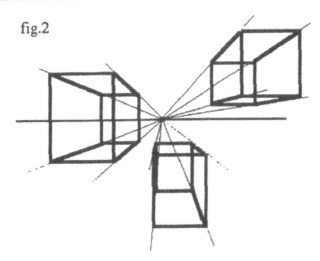

fig.2

The length of the cubes is set when you establish the smaller far end of the cube.

In fig.3, I started shading the sides of the cubes. This makes it easier to see. Note that the left side of the lowest box is barely visible. This is because you are looking right down the edge of the cube. Also note, the cube above the vanishing point, you can see its bottom and the cube below the vanishing point you can see its top. This is because the vanishing point represents your eye level in the picture, just like it did in the two point perspective discussed earlier.

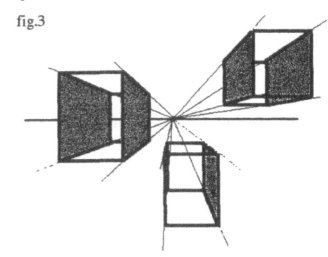

fig.3

Fig.4 has all four sides of the cube shaded.

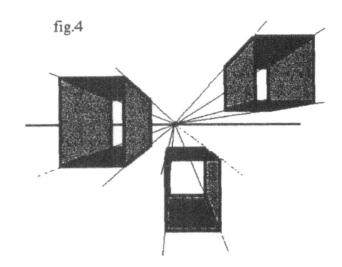

fig.4

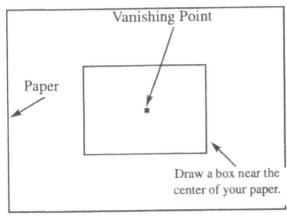

Draw lines from the vanishing point to the edge of the paper.

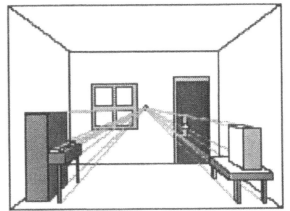

Draw lines from the corners of the rectangle that represents the near end of your TV to the vanishing point.

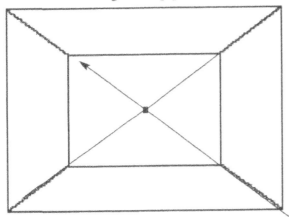

Draw a door and a window in the box you drew. Then draw the near edge of some objects in your room such as a TV or piano.

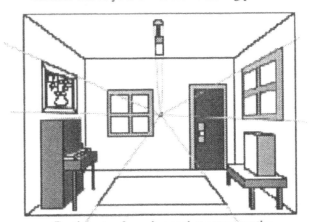

Continue to place shapes that represent the near ends of objects in your room, and then draw very light lines to the vanishing point.

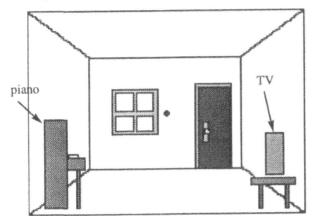

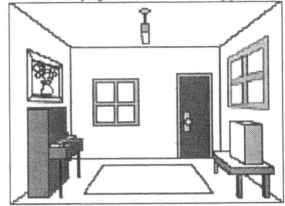

These construction lines should be very light because they will need to be erased in the final picture.

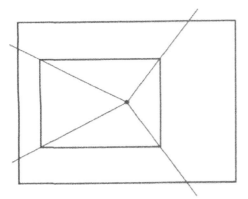

NOTE!! If the box is not drawn exactly in the center of the page, (which is most often the case), the vanishing point lines will not go to the corner of the page. This will not hurt anything and sometimes this can be used to give the picture an interesting effect. The lines must be drawn from the vanishing point through the corners of the box you have drawn, not the page corners. Draw a line from the vanishing point through the corner of the box you have drawn and onward to the edge of the page.

35

fig.1

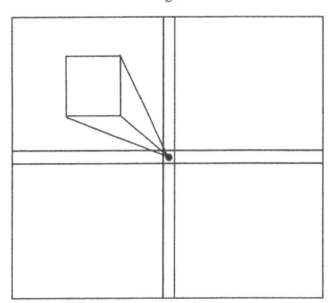

The vanishing point represents the eye level in any picture. It is the place you are looking in the picture. What if you were looking straight down? Looking straight down from a very tall building sometimes makes people sick, so be careful. Place a street intersection in the shape of an "X" or "T" on your paper. It is often more interesting to place it off center of the page. You can see in fig.1 the streets are in the very center. This makes for a poor composition. In fig.2, I tilted the streets and placed them off center. This makes for a more interesting picture but will be a little harder to accomplish. When you do this kind of picture, you can start with the streets. The size or width of these streets determines how high your buildings are. A wide street makes you nearer the ground and the narrower the street the higher the building looks. One problem, if you get too high it is difficult to see the sidewalks, or cars. Also very tall buildings make it hard to see any separations between the bases of the buildings.

Draw the streets and then put a vanishing point in the center, where the streets meet.

One thing that you need to make sure of is that the tops of the buildings need to be parallel to the streets. An easy way to do the buildings is to draw the top of the building and then draw lines from the corner of the roof

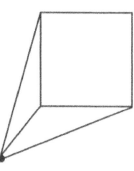

top to the vanishing point. This is even easier than the first lesson, where you drew three cubes. It is easier because you don't even need a horizon line.

See the next page for the complete city.

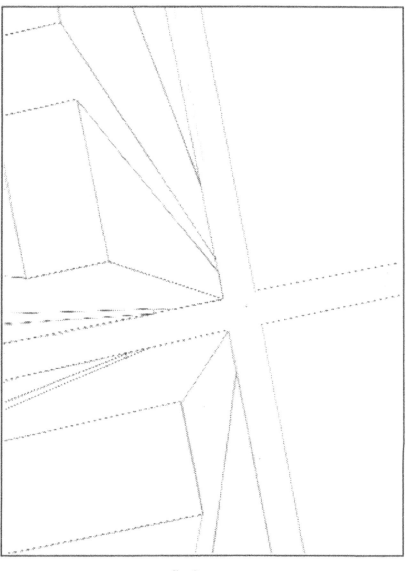

fig.2

36

Notice how the buildings are just cubes with bases near the vanishing point.

Now we will turn our view of our one point perspective so we are looking far into the distant horizon. Notice on this picture everything gets closer together, even the clouds get smaller and closer together as they get farther away. If this were a painting, I would make things in the distance lighter, and everything darker and brighter as it gets nearer. That would be called atmosphere perspective.

I will do one more one point perspective. On the following page is an object drawn in one point from two different angles. One angle is above the horizon and one below.

fig.1

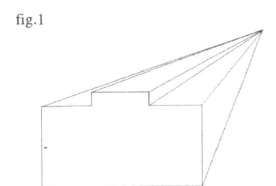

fig.2

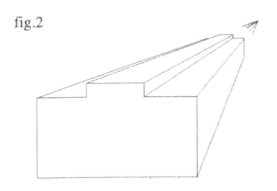

The horizon lines in both fig.3 and fig.5 are established by the vanishing points in those pictures.

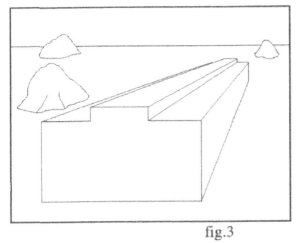

fig.3

Notice that the lines going to the vanishing point are hidden by either the ark itself, or the mountain it is resting on.

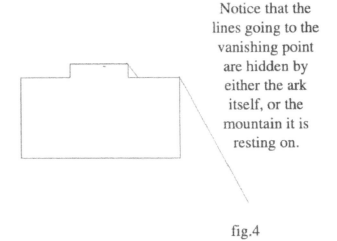

fig.4

Noah's Ark was 75 feet wide, 45 feet tall and 450 feet long. It was probably a rectangle. It didn't have a bow, rudder or sails. It did not need to go anywhere. God was in charge. Just like He is in the life of a believer who in in the spiritual ark of Jesus.

It is simple to show something wide and tall, but to make something look long is a different matter. Here the use of a vanishing point gives the ark length. The vanishing point represents the eye level of the person looking at the picture. If it is below the ark, you have to look up to it, and if it is above, you are looking down on top.

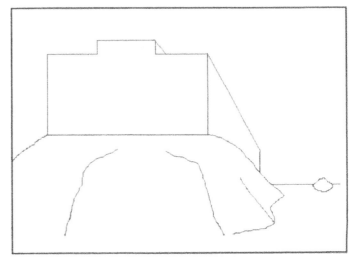

fig.5

All of the proceeding examples of drawing perspectives have been out of my imagination. Now we will try a couple of real life situations. Recently, I had to pick up someone at the airport. Their plane was late arriving because the plane already at the terminal wouldn't leave. I had two minutes to spend so I took out my sketch pad and drew what I saw. This turned out to be a plane ready to leave with the ramp door already retracted, but the plane still hooked to the ground electrical source. As I drew this picture, I knew I only had a few seconds. I first attempted drawing the plane using a one point. I had a little trouble because as I looked out of the terminal window it was difficult determining at what level to place the vanishing point. When I started drawing, I quickly noticed that I had picked a wrong point and the plane was coming out viewed from a different angle. The apparent angle was more along the side of the aircraft. This is a very common mistake I see in my students. I had to start over. On the second

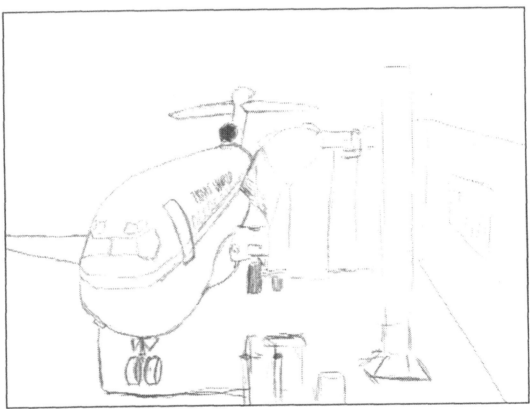

attempt, I decided to draw the entry ramp first. This was because it wasn't in the perspective plain. It was like the end wall of a one point perspective room. All of its lines were either horizontal or vertical. After I had this drawn, it was easy to place the one point airplane beside the movable ramp. I could see that the wing of the airplane was just above the bottom of the ramp, and I could see the tires. I could also see that the tail appeared above the ramp, but below the support column. After I had all of these reference points, I was able to place the vanishing point in the proper place. Something else I noticed as I raced through this picture is that I have a tendency, like many of my students, to draw vertical lines that are slanted. Most often they are slanted to the right at the top. I mention this because it is something you as an artist will need to be aware of and correct. In this case, I didn't notice it until later. It looked good to me, because I had drawn it like I thought it was, but later when I looked down the edge of my paper and the vertical lines of my sketch didn't match with the edge of the paper, I knew it wasn't right. One thing I do sometimes is to hold up the paper to a light and look at it from its back. If anything is slanted, it will be very noticeable.

40

This drawing of an old house in my town is an example of a real life two point perspective. Actually this is the place where we hold our annual art camp. It is called "The Bonebrake Center of Nature and History."

one hand and sight over its edge so that it appears to run along the roof line of the building. Notice where this line hits your horizon line. Do the same thing with the foundations. Note the natural vanishing points and the angles they make with

When drawing something like this , it is important to set the vanishing points in the proper place. To do this, look straight and level at the building. Find a place on the building that is even with your eye. That place is on your horizon line. The vanishing points are along that line. One common mistake is to place the points too close together. Another mistake made is to try to make the building too large. This is probably because you are sitting in front of this huge building, and because it almost fills your field of vision. This is really only a problem if you have already placed your vanishing points on the edge of your paper. If you have a large building, you will need the vanishing points well off of the page. One way to help get it right, is to hold up a ruler or straight edge with

the horizon line. Place these angles on you horizon line on your paper. These lines will determine the height of the corner nearest you. Using this, your building will turn out closer to the right size. Note also if I would have walked twenty feet to my left, this picture would have been a one point and not a two point. I also opted to place the tree in front of the building. I had several reasons. One, it really was there and is part of the beauty of the place, and two, it hid some of the windows and I was using it as a reference point i.e. I could see some of two windows that I was measuring with the width of the tree. I also chose to leave off many of the tree leaves. I felt they hid too much of the picture.

LESSON 6
Drawing The Face

Students often tell me that they can draw anything except people. I tell them that drawing the human face can be made a little easier if they learn the classic proportions of the face. Faces of people have been in the same proportions throughout all of history. You can measure ancient statues or paintings from long extinct civilizations and the proportions are always the same. Some say that people are getting taller and this may be true in general but even at that, the proportions of their faces haven't changed. The problem about drawing faces is you really have to study details. If I draw two eyes, a nose, a mouth, two ears, and some hair it doesn't make it anybody. I have to take the time to draw specific eyes, nose, ears and all the rest. It isn't any face; it is a specific face. THE DIFFERENCE IS IN THE DETAILS!!!! Every head is a different shape. Every eye is unique. Every nose is unlike any other..

The reason students have such a difficult time with faces is if it isn't just like the person you are drawing, it really looks wrong. We, as humans, have an ability to recognize others by their faces. We sometimes see someone that will remind us of someone else, but on closer inspection the differences come out. It is these little differences that make the difference in face drawing. Below are the classic proportions of the face. They are guidelines to place roughly where the features go. I can tell you they are approximately where you will find the facial features on most people. But everybody is different and each feature needs to be analyzed and set in relationship with every other on each individual's face. Below you can see that most people have heads five times the width of their eye. Also notice that the mouth is as wide as the center of the eyes. Ears go between the eye line and the nose line and the rest is hair.

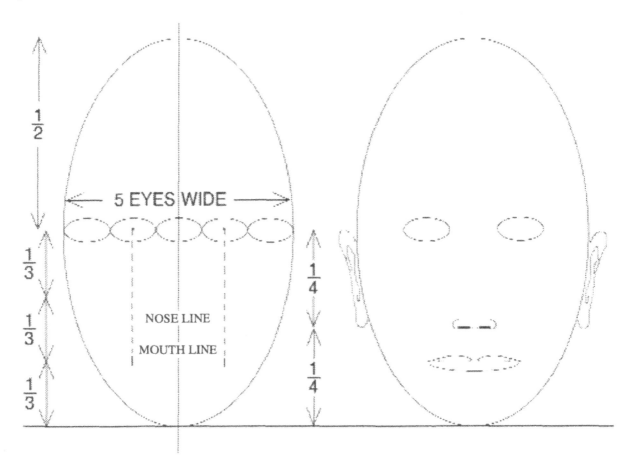

fig.1

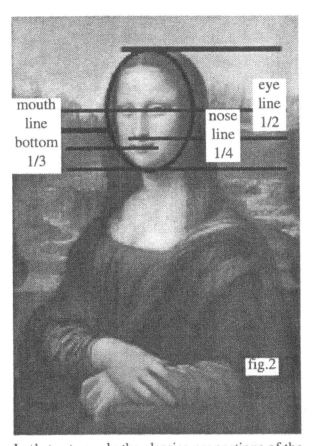

mouth line bottom 1/3

nose line 1/4

eye line 1/2

fig.2

Let's try to apply the classics proportions of the face to this well known painting from the Renaissance. We can see (fig.2) that Mona's face is in the same proportions as yours. In (fig.3), we can see that her head is slightly turned to her right. This turning of her head makes it difficult to see that her head is five eyes wide. You can see though, that there is an eye's width between her two eyes; and her famous smile is as wide as the center of her eyes.

fig.3

What I would like for you to notice on this young lady is that her head is slightly tilted to your left.

This can only be seen by drawing lines through the center of her eyes and down her nose.

There are two ways to draw a face. The first and most common is to use the classic proportions of the face, (see page 37). (The second method will be discussed later). When you try this first method, the first thing you should do is determine the overall shape of the head. Some people have heads that are round, some oval, some narrower on the top and wider on the chin and visa versa. Some are just plain block headed. You start with this shape, layout the spaces for the eyes, nose, mouth, etc and then look for details that make the differences.

This method of using proportions is only a general outline. You will not often find a person that has all of the average features. They also will have their head turned or tilted as this woman does

which makes some of the measurements difficult to determine. Look at this woman. She has an eye's width between her eyes, but doesn't have an eye's width from her right eye to the side of her head. There are two eye's width next to her left eye. All of this is due to the turning of her head. There is an advantage to having a face turned. The picture is sometimes more interesting, and as the head is turned the nose gets more of an edge. This edge makes the nose easier to define and shape.

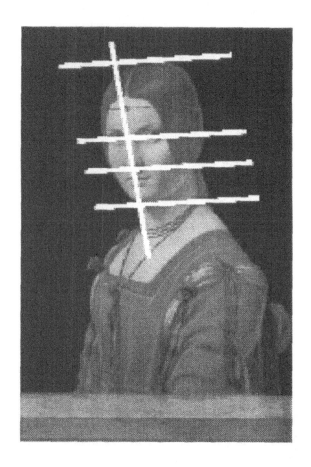

44

For practice, I want you to tear a photograph out of a magazine.such as the one in fig.1.

Take the picture and draw a line directly down the center of the face. Fold the photograph down this line and tape it onto your drawing paper. As shown in fig.2.

fig.2

Now complete the drawing of the face. Draw the remainder of the face by coping the side that you see. Don't try to imagine what the side looks like that you can't see just copy what you do see. Look at the example in fig.3. Notice that it doesn't look like the original photograph. This is due mostly to the change of the hair by having both sides alike, but it is also due to the fact that both eyes are not the same in the photograph but are in the drawing.

After you complete this side you can turn the photograph over and do the other side. When this is complete you will have a mirror image of the original photograph, which is best viewed in a mirror.

fig.3

Remember, it is important to get the basic entire shape, and leave the detail for later. Don't get lost in the detail and loose the whole picture.

45

I said earlier there was two methods of drawing the face. The second way is to draw one eye, then to use that eye as a grid piece to determine the rest of the face. Using the measuring techniques

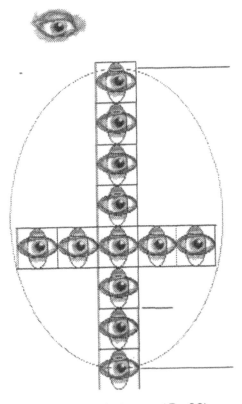

described in Lesson 4, (pages 17 - 22), measure the spaces between the eyes, length of the nose and placement of the ears and mouth. Lightly draw them in and then measure the width of the face and hair.

One exercise that is very helpful to learn how to draw a face is to draw your own face. Sit down next to a mirror and draw your face.

In this practice, sit close to a mirror and start drawing your facial features. Start by drawing one of your eyes. Look very close at just one eye. Look at the overall shape; then the eye itself. Draw it very lightly. See how the lines run around and form the eye lid. Copy the eye in as great detail as possible. Complete the eye by stroking on the eye lashes. If the eye isn't up to your satisfaction draw it again.

Remember, PRACTICE, PRACTICE, PRACTICE. After you are satisfied the eye is just like the one in the mirror, try drawing your nose. Look at the holes in the end of your nose. Drawing the nostril and the flaps of skin that go around them is the most important thing in drawing noses. There are no sharp edges in a nose, the rest of the nose is shadow or shading. The width of the nose is shown by how wide apart the nostrils are and the length is determined by where on the face you start drawing the nose and by how dark a shadow there is. If the shadow is so long you could use it as a sundial, the nose is very long. After you have the nose just like you want it, try to draw your lips. Now draw the rest of your face, one piece at a time. This is PRACTICE. You will need to do this several times so that you can get a little faster. It takes a little speed before you are ready to try to draw someone else. You are the probably the only person that can sit still long enough for you practice drawing a portrait. Most people won't sit still for it.

A quick two minute sketch of a student.

46

A variation of the previous exercise is to try to do an unusual self portrait. Look at various self portraits by other artists. Some of my favorite are Norman Rockwell's, (he has himself as the artist peering over his glasses at the mirror, painting his portrait which has him beaming with perfection). M.C. Escher's, (he is looking into a mirror ball and not only did the artist draw his portrait, but you can see his hand and the rest of his world where he lived reflected in the ball). There are many others to look at because most artists have drawn their self portraits. You can even try to copy them. Copying the master works is a very good way to learn. This exercise, however, is for you to be creative, original and unique. Try to draw your self portrait in a way nobody else has ever tried.

Two more quick sketches, just for practice.

Once you have practiced by drawing yourself, start asking your friends to sit still while you draw. Find someone who wants to learn to draw along with you and you can draw them and they can draw you. Don't worry if it doesn't look just like the person, remember this is practice. Your friend needs to understand that the picture isn't a statement of how you feel about them or any political reasons, it is just a practice!

Try to draw several people in different positions and using different methods. Try to draw them up close and then farther back. You also may want to just draw their eye, nose, mouth, ear or hair separately. Drawing just one part is especially helpful if you seem to have problems drawing some particular part such as noses. If you do have trouble with something, it will always help to practice. Several other points: One, if you have to draw teeth, it is better to mute them out and make teeth less pronounced. If you draw the teeth as well defined and bright, the picture will look somewhat like a vampire or Cheshire Cat. Two, if the person is wearing glasses, it is best to draw the eyes first and then the glasses last. Three, for me it is best to draw the hair by looking at the outline first, and then follow several hairs as to its direction and the stroke in the rest, looking for dark shadows and highlights.

Last, it is a good exercise to learn to draw cloth. Set up some old shirt or towel and draw it in as great detail as you can. This is a difficult thing to do, but is good practice. This will come in very handy when you start drawing the clothes people are wearing.

47

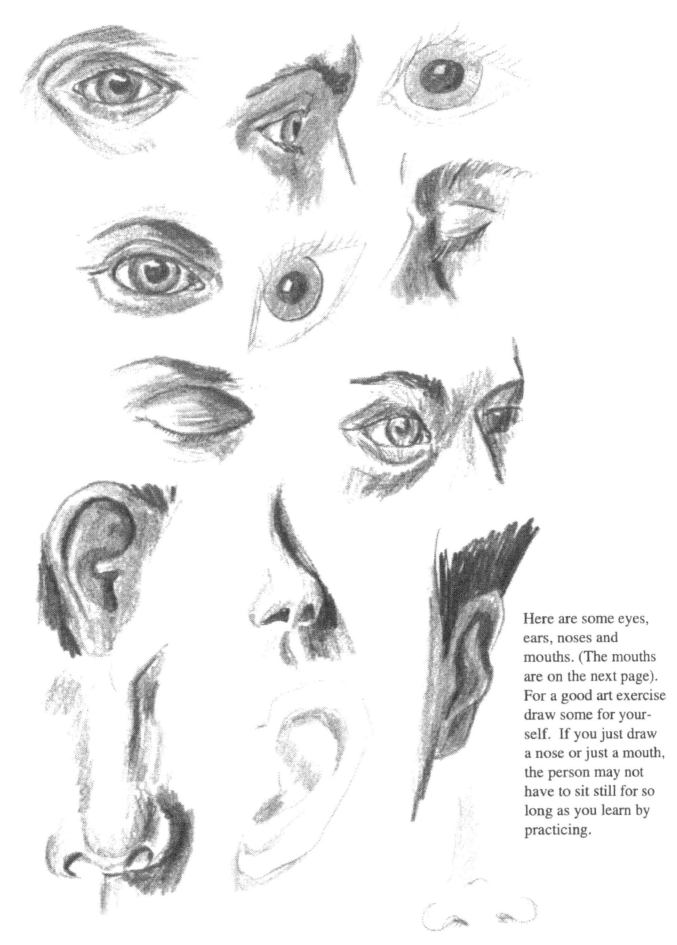

Here are some eyes, ears, noses and mouths. (The mouths are on the next page). For a good art exercise draw some for yourself. If you just draw a nose or just a mouth, the person may not have to sit still for so long as you learn by practicing.

There is a little crease of skin that runs from the bottom of the nose to the top of the mouth called a philtrum. Not everybody has one; only about 99% of the population. The philtrum is mentioned because as you can see, it forms the little "U" shape in the top lip. It also disappears when you smile. As the lips spread in a broad smile, the skin gets tight and the philtrum disappears. It is something to look for when drawing portraits. Some people have very sharp well pronounced philtrums, and some you can scarcely see.

49

The thing I love most about looking at a work by Auguste Renoir, is the bright and joyful way he painted. Even when he was in great pain with arthritis, his work exhibited much joy. It is said that there was a time when his sons would tie a paintbrush in his hands in order for him to paint. It is wonderful to read about his courage and the way he wanted to bring beauty into peoples' lives. There is a story that the great artist Matisse came to see him and asked, "Why do you paint, Auguste, when it seems to cause you so much pain?" Renoir was reported to have replied "The beauty is worth the pain." Look at this lovely picture of a child. Did you know that the head is larger in proportion to the body in a child then in an adult? An adult's body is about 7 1/2 times the size of the head. In this picture, you can see that the child's body is 4 1/2 times as large as her head. The younger the child is, the larger the head is in proportion to the body. Choose a particular age child, and then draw the child and an adult in the picture with them.

Draw a baby or small child.

Notice how this baby is only as long as three of his heads, if they were stacked one on the other.

50

You can see the difference between an adult and a child by this picture. The mother is only three heads long to her waist but the daughter is only a total of four heads tall.

I wanted to end this study of portraits by looking at one of the masters. In the analysis below, you can see that Van Gogh used the classic proportions to do his self portrait; his face was really quite normal.

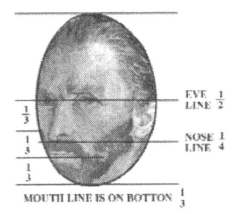

51

Jeffus (order #332044)

LESSON 7

Drawing people in motion.

We discussed figure drawing in a previous lesson. We talked about the head being used as a unit of measure to determine the size of a person's body. Here we are going to expand on the figure drawing and add some movement. Movement is generally shown by diagonal lines. This is easily seen in sports pictures, but you can see the use of diagonal lines to show movement almost anywhere. If you look at the picture *Breezing Up* by Winslow Homer, you can see the use of diagonal lines to show movement of a sailboat. If you think about a picture with the sailboat masts standing straight up and the water perfectly flat, the picture wouldn't have much movement; only stillness. But the picture sailboat masts in the picture *Breezing Up* , are all leaning with the wind and the water is in turmoil.

Cartoon car
at rest.

Cartoon car moving at high speed. The only real difference is the diagonal lines.

When I need an action figure, I get one of my children to pose. Many times I will place them in some awkward position and try to keep them still as I draw. I've also used friends and some art stu-

dents. This, however, isn't always easy. People sometimes don't want to stand perfectly still as they stand on their tip toes pointing skyward. I know a young man who does Christian super hero comic books. His art work has many dramatic figures with bulging muscles. The figures are very realistic. When I ask him how he learned to do such great muscle structures, I thought he would have studied medical books of muscles or some advanced drawing book, but instead he told me he practiced by drawing action figure dolls like GI Joe and The Incredible Hulk. What a great idea!! The muscles on these dolls are exaggerated but anatomically correct. Most of these type of dolls can be posed in action and don't really mind standing still for long periods of time. Besides that, you can get them inexpensively at yard sales. You can get them cheaper than the artist models that are much more costly and often don't have muscles.

Even with all that said, it still is a good idea to get a book of anatomy and study both bones and muscles. I should caution you here. Many art books use nudes to study the form of the human body. This may be relevant for some books and maybe for some older students, but I haven't found it to be essential. Practically speaking, in most commercial art the people are fully clothed. If you need to draw a car with a model standing next to it, the model will be clothed. Most people in shopping malls, airports and other public places have clothing on. So, for everyday drawing it is more practical to learn to draw clothing than it is to learn to draw nudes. Whether people have clothes on or not, their arms are on the same place of their body and their knees bend the same. The most important thing to study is how humans bend and move.

54

Here is a skeleton. If you wanted to, you could learn the names of every bone. It would make you a better artist if you learned their placement, relative length, or how they bend one to another. What you should study first is where the fingers fall when the hand is by the side and the length of each major body part in "heads"

Here you see the chest is two heads high and the upper leg from the hip joint to the knee is two an one half heads.

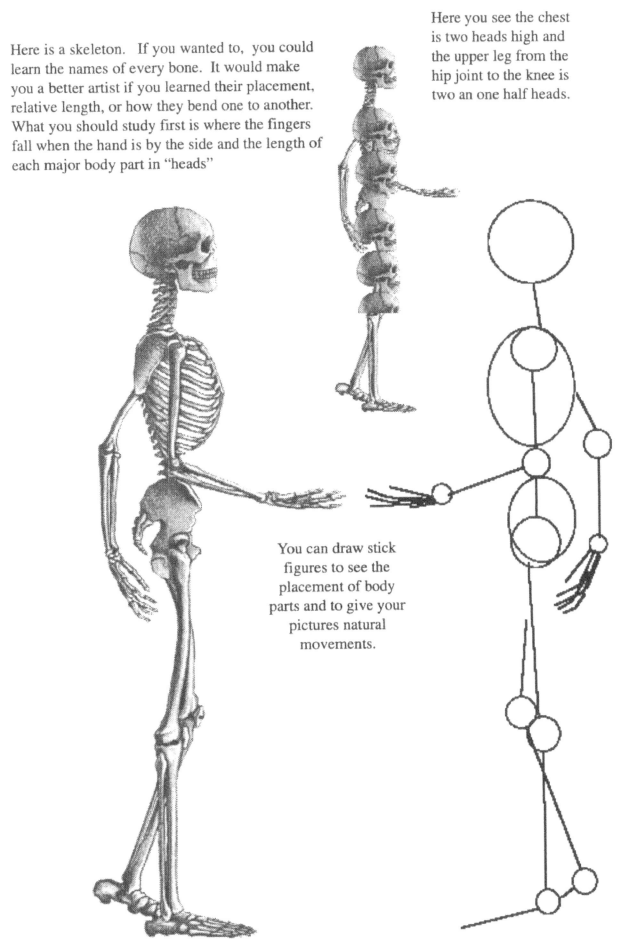

You can draw stick figures to see the placement of body parts and to give your pictures natural movements.

Here are some muscles to look at. There are many books that have similar pictures. Leonardo da Vinci was one of the first artists interested in the inside of the body. His anatomical drawings were used in the fields of art and medicine for many years.

This arm, (fig.2) is the same arm as shown in fig.1. I have put the skin on to show how it would look. It is a little exaggerated in shape because I wanted to stress the muscles. I left off the fat that normally rounds out the flesh and makes it smoother.

fig.2

Fig.3 is my arm as I see it in a mirror. Just kidding. I have taken the same arm from fig.1 and even more exaggerated it to show making muscles is easy, once you know where they go.

fig.3

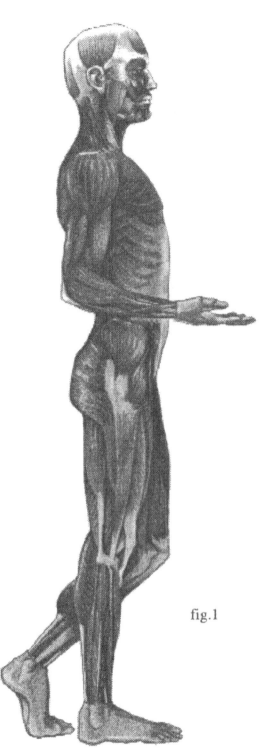

fig.1

Fig.5 is skin over the muscles in the back of the leg. Fig.4 is more like a leg really looks. Note that the pair of calf muscles, shown in fig 5, are filled in with flesh making the appearance of one muscle. It is important to remember as you study the muscle structure, that the flesh, fat, and veins all add to a more realistic looking figure.

fig.5

fig.4

The idea of knowing the names of the bones as a way of studying their place, length and relative size is applicable to the muscle structures. Names are important, if you are trying to communicate with someone else who knows the names. Other wise, it is important to study how they bend and shape the body.

56

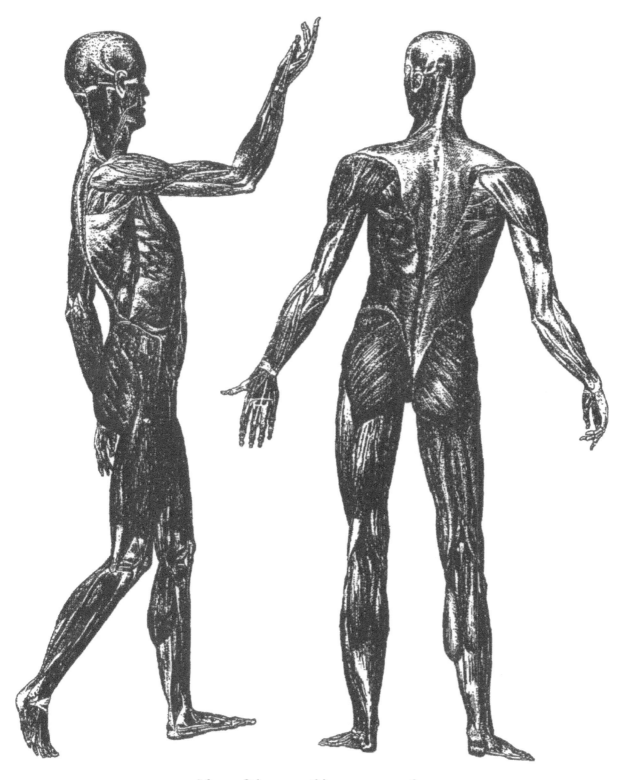

More of the same thing one more time.

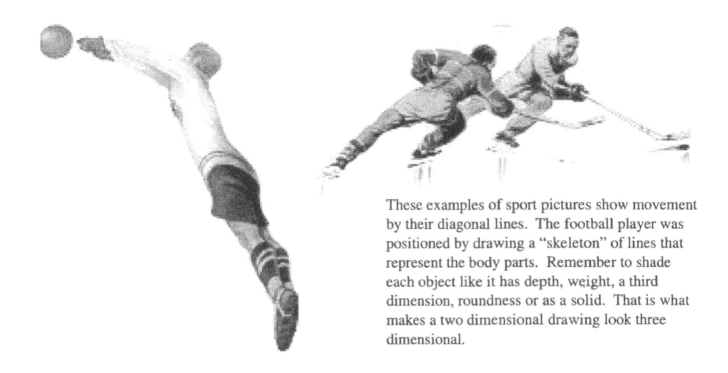

These examples of sport pictures show movement by their diagonal lines. The football player was positioned by drawing a "skeleton" of lines that represent the body parts. Remember to shade each object like it has depth, weight, a third dimension, roundness or as a solid. That is what makes a two dimensional drawing look three dimensional.

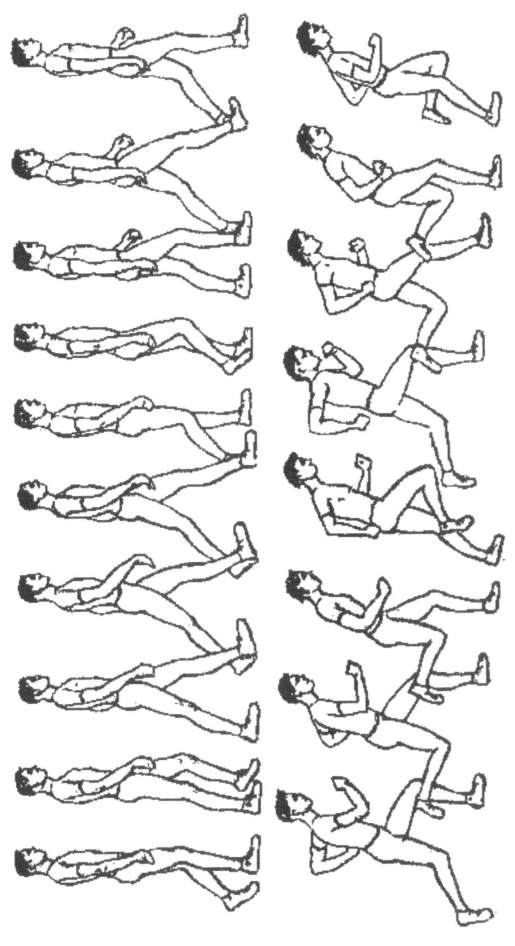

This is an example of motion. Study how the person is moving. Watch people walk or as you walk, observe how you move. Your back is slightly bent and your weight is centered over the foot that is grounded. As your left foot goes forward, so does your right hand and vice versa. It is important to draw people walking. It is often necessary to put people in your pictures and if they are walking, the people don't look stiff or posed. If you can learn to draw people walking, people running is easy. Running is just exaggerated walking. You lean as you walk, but more so when you run. You bend your legs when you walk, but more so when you run. The same thing with the length of your stride or the flexing of the muscles. Practice drawing people walking. First use stick figures and then fill them in.

59

Still Life

Still life drawing is drawing an arrangement of inanimate objects. Only part of the picture is the subject. The rest of the picture is in its execution; or how the picture is laid out or designed.

Good pictures don't just happen, they are planned. When you study a great artist like Michaelango or Leonardo da Vinci, you find that they often did many preliminary sketches before attempting to do a finished work. These artists were trying to find out what works. They needed to determine the shape of each individual piece of the picture and how each piece influenced other pieces. The artist wanted to control the eyes of the person looking at the picture. They want to make the person look first here, and then there, and always keeping the attention on the picture never wandering off.

If you have two children of unequal weight, the heavier one has to be closer to the center to balance. This is called asymmetrical or informal balance. This is the same in art but the weight of the objects is composed of size, color and contrast. As an example, a small, dark, bright red object has more weight than a larger, dull object. Because it attracts more attention.

The next time you are looking at paintings by the masters, look at their use of red. This can be seen in many pictures or prints, but it really is best to go to the art museum and see the originals. This is because sometimes the artist will only use a tiny flick of red somewhere on the painting. This tiny speck doesn't always show up in a reproduction. The artist uses this little flash of color to draw the eyes to the center of interest in the picture.

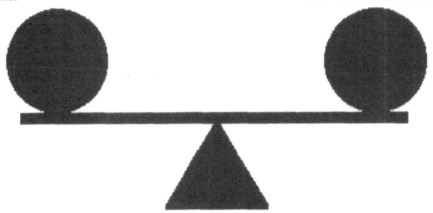

I will briefly discuss some of the elements you may need to consider in order to produce a well designed picture.

Balance

Like children on a seesaw, so is balance in a picture. If you have two children of equal weight on both ends, that is formal balance.

Rhythm

Rhythm can be established with line, color, value and shape. If lines are all the same width and length, the picture may be balanced but boring. Varying the components of a picture makes the picture more interesting. It is the rhythm of the picture. The rhythm is similar to that of music. The variations of line, color, value and shape give the picture almost a musical form. The same note played over and over again is boring, monotonous and can even be irritating. When the artist varies the rhythm, adds color, increases or decreases the contrast and has a wide range of shape the painting becomes more like an orchestra playing beautiful music.

Generally variety is the spice of life. The more variety in a picture the more interesting the picture. This is not always the case in every picture but is a rule of thumb. In some pictures, the artist may want to change this as a statement, or to better illustrate what he is trying to communicate.

Value

Value is the intensity of a color or a contrast of gray tones. Value, is also that use of a gradation from dark to light and has been used up to now to define shape and give substance to realistic drawings. Now we are going to discuss value as a component of a design. Notice how mush more the dark circle draws your eye than the lighter circle of the same size? Some designs don't occupy a space. These are designs like logos, patterns or other illustrations often used in commercial art to bring beauty to everyday objects;for instance patterns on clothing or carpets. This kind of design also adorns engraved objects like jewelry or glass work. This type of design does not need a light source and the intent isn't to be realistic. Value in design is needed to separate objects, give line, and help set up the rhythm.

This lamp made an interesting study. It could be considered a still life. Most still life's have an odd number of components. Such as one, three, five and seven. If the still life contains more elements than that, they are usually looked at in groups of elements.

This piece was fun to do because of the glass. Making the lamp base transparent was simple. I concentrated on the dark areas and made sure to leave the highlights. Like any other representational drawing, the more details you can manage, the better the picture usually looks.

62

This still life is somewhat more complicated. The flowers themselves are small and numerous. I did my sketch of this artist's painting using an ebony drawing pencil. I also simplified the picture by leaving out some of the background folded material.

In doing still life, composition is of the utmost importance. Because composition lends interest to a picture, the way you display your apples and peaches, your lovely vase, or your collection of interesting books is so very important. You want to have an odd number of items on an irregular level.

63

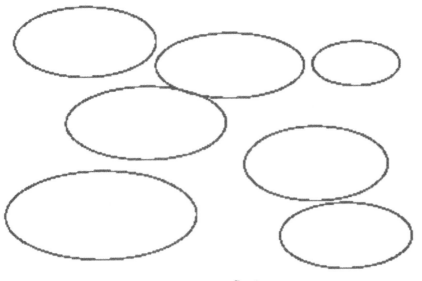

In fig.1 the circles represent several of the same type of objects, such as apples or pastries, in fig.3 the circles represent groups of diverse objects in fig.4. I use this to illustrate that, even though the pictures look complex, they are arranged in a relatively small number of uneven groups.

fig.1

This is an example of a still life with an odd number of groups of objects. If you were to count each object in a group as an individual, you get a number that is unusable. As you see in fig.1, each of the circles represent many different individual objects in fig.2

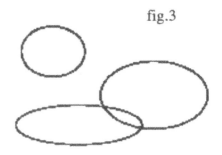

fig.3

fig.4

fig.2

Everybody likes roses. This was
chosen from another artist's work
and changed slightly. I simplified
the background. I liked this drawing because of the unique vase. It
has an unusual way the light
shines off of it.

Joffus (order #332044)

Here, I have placed a line on the top of each bottle and one down the center line of the bottle. Notice how they are all on different elevations and are of different lengths. Also, notice that the artist did not make all of the bottles standing perfectly straight up.

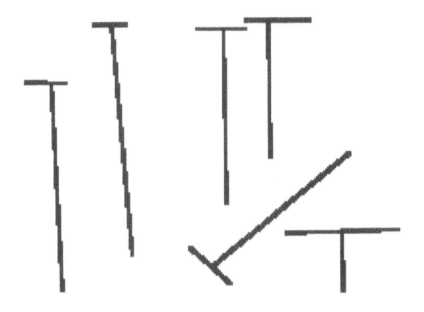

66

Notice how the artist uses the curves to direct the eyes to the center of this picture.

This still life is interesting because the artist uses a complicated background to augment this complex painting.

67

LESSON 9

Drawing Animals

In previous chapters of this book, several different methods of drawing are discussed. These methods when practiced can be used effectively to draw anything. Defining the space with circles, using contour lines, shading and shadows to define the shape and the use of texture to give the picture its finish look, are some of techniques you should have practiced before now. We also have covered the grid, the implied grid, and the use of a small part such as an eye to "measure" the rest of the picture.

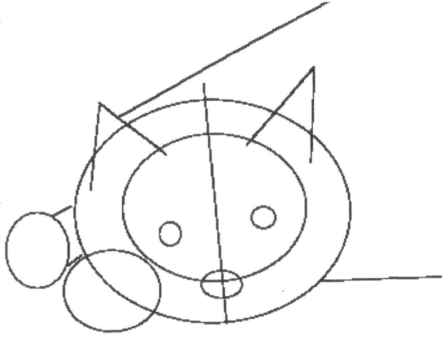

When doing animals you may need all of the above skills along with the lessons on muscles and motion.

Remember the eyes of the animal are very important. Leave a little bit of white in the eye to show the reflection of light.

68

This is an example of creating a different picture by taking an existing picture and changing it . This raccoon was drawn by using basic shapes to occupy the space; contour line to define the shape; shading to give the form substance and finally the hair was stroked on for texture.

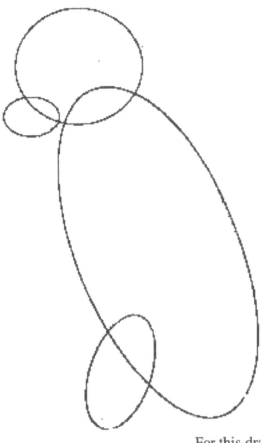

For this drawing I first used circles to define space, then a contour line to define shape, and then finally shading to give form.

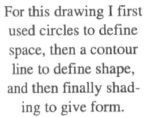

70

Contour Outline Drawing

Start the drawing by doing a
continuous outline drawing

Completed outline

Outlines of the shadows
and high lights are
added.

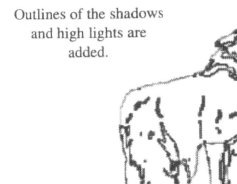

The coyote is completed
by shading and shadow.

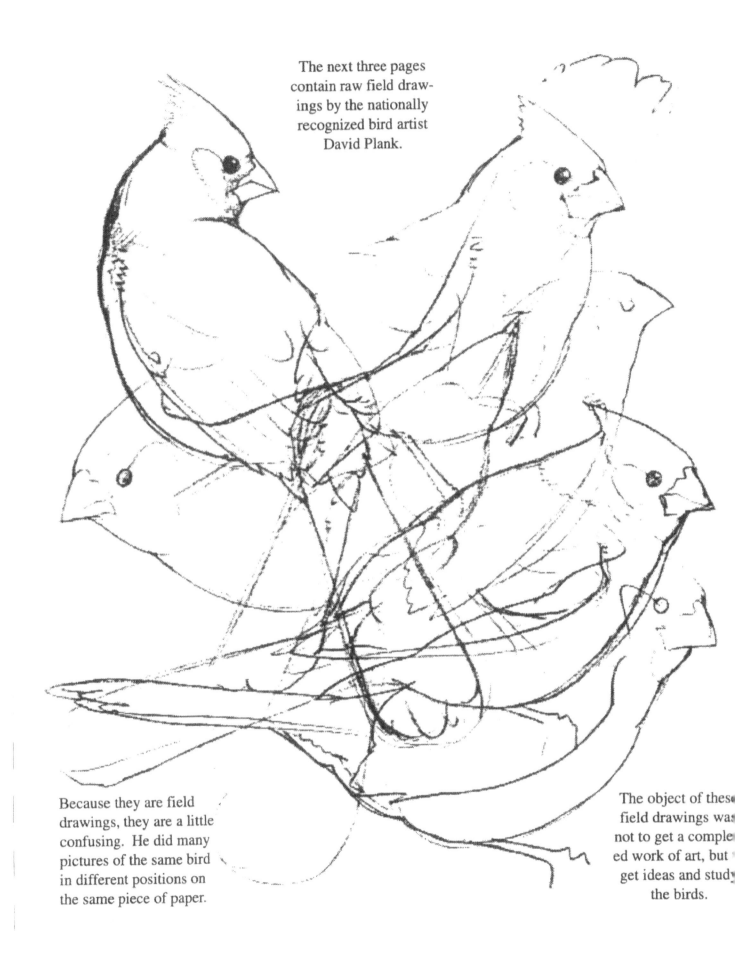

The next three pages contain raw field drawings by the nationally recognized bird artist David Plank.

Because they are field drawings, they are a little confusing. He did many pictures of the same bird in different positions on the same piece of paper.

The object of these field drawings was not to get a completed work of art, but to get ideas and study the birds.

Notice how David writes on the field sketches to
help him remember the environment where he studied the birds, habitat, time and place.

Any detail is important to
the final picture.

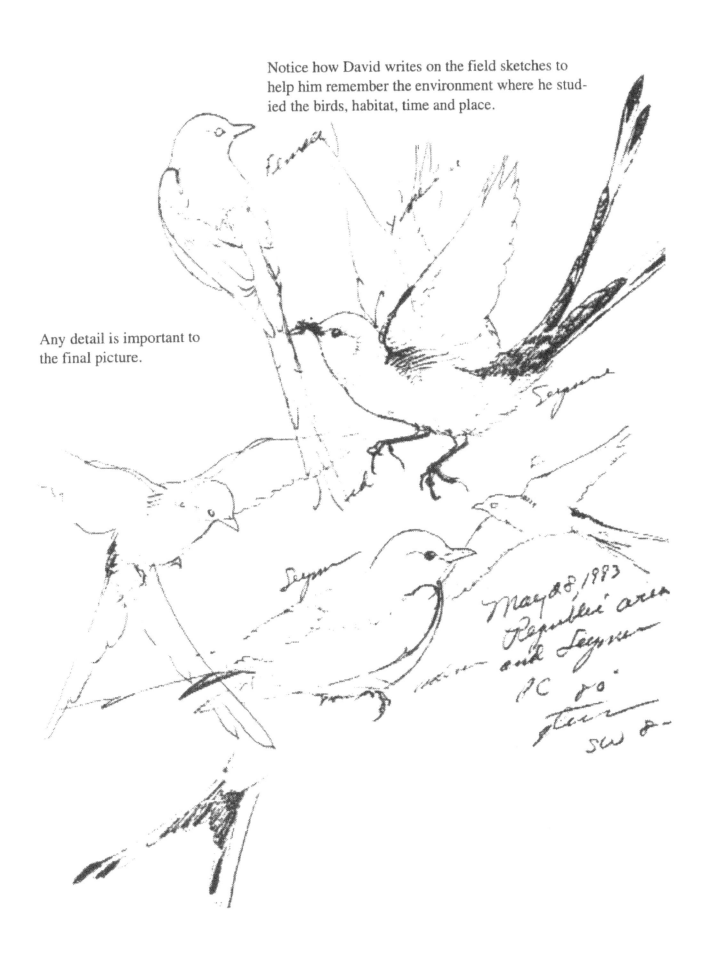

CARTOONS AND CARICATURE

At the bottom of this page is a cartoon. Cartoons and caricature, (caricature by definition is a picture or imitation of a person with certain features exaggerated for satirical effect) have several things in common. The way you do either is to find a feature and exaggerate it. If a person has a large chin, you make it huge. If the person has big ears, you draw them gigantic. Cartoons are similar because they are generally exaggerated stereotypes. For example, a cartoon rabbit would have very long ears.

Next time you have an opportunity to study pictures of that famous cartoon rabbit, I know you could name, look at his ears. They are nearly as long as one third of his entire body length. A real rabbit's ears are actually shorter than the length of its head. In the same way if you want to draw a pirate cartoon, he might have a patch on one eye and a peg leg. A computer geek might have thick glasses, a pocket pen protector, and a crooked tie. The stereotypes are endless,

and although they are often inaccurate, they are the best way to communicate what you want.

Below the cartoon of the raccoon picks up on the raccoon 's mask. The mask is a stereotype for a bandit or robber. I used that stereotype to make the raccoon look like he is stealing something.

LESSON 10

Landscapes

Taking your sketchbook outside and doing outdoor nature drawing is probably the best way to learn to draw landscapes. You can learn a variety of flora and fauna by just carefully observing and drawing them; see the next page for some tree shapes. When drawing landscapes, you will use many of the techniques that you have already practiced. If you are outside and attempting to draw a scene such as a view of a valley or some other expanse, it is easier if you start by drawing some single object like a single tree or house. Once you have this object, you can use it to measure the rest of the scene. Using this method, it is easy to get the right proportions. When drawing outdoors, a common mistake is to get the picture out of proportion. Another concern is when you are drawing landscapes, seascapes or even cityscapes, you will need to give your pictures both mathematical and atmospheric perspective. Mathematical or linear perspective was covered thoroughly in the lesson on perspective. Atmospheric perspective is the apparent reduction of contrast and colour of objects in the distance. This is easy to explain if you think about what you see when you look far away.

If you are fortunate to live in an area of the country with mountains, or have ever went on a trip to the mountains, this is easier to explain. The mountains in the far distance are almost light blue. As each closer mountain range overlaps the one in back of it, it becomes darker and brighter. The nearest to you is bright and full of colour. This same phenomenon occurs with the sky. On the horizon line the sky is light blue, almost the same colour as the distant mountains. As you look higher and higher into the sky, the sky gets a deeper and deeper colour of blue. If there are clouds present, they get brighter and brighter white. This color contrast is caused by atmospheric conditions. Things such as water vapor and dust cause the distant light to be absorbed. The mathematical or linear perspective is apparent in the outdoor scenes also. The clouds in the sky appear smaller and smaller as they run toward the horizon. This is easy to see if the clouds are a layer of puffy white cumulus clouds. These clouds will also overlap each cloud that is farther away. This same overlapping will take place with each mountain or tree as you look farther and farther away.

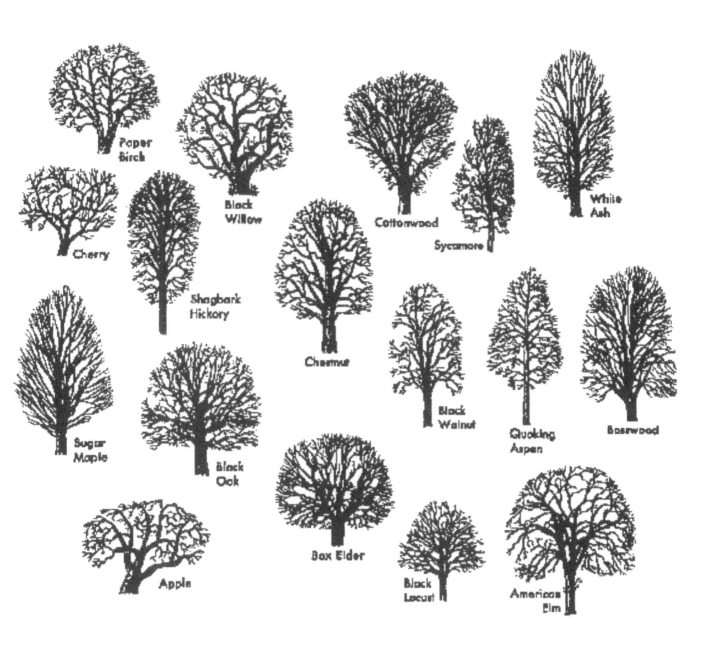

Paper Birch

Cherry

Black Willow

Shagbark Hickory

Cottonwood

Sycamore

White Ash

Chestnut

Sugar Maple

Black Oak

Box Elder

Black Walnut

Quaking Aspen

Basswood

Apple

Black Locust

American Elm

Drawing trees is an important part of almost any landscape. Above are a few tree shapes. It is easiest to learn their shapes during the winter, when they have lost their leaves. In general, broad leaf trees such as oaks and hickories are round shapes, and conifers such as pines and fir are cone shapes.

Oak

What you have learned about texture will hold true in landscape drawing. In no other topic are you able to use such great variety in creating texture. Use your pencil to make squiggly lines for the trees. Use stroking lines for the bark.

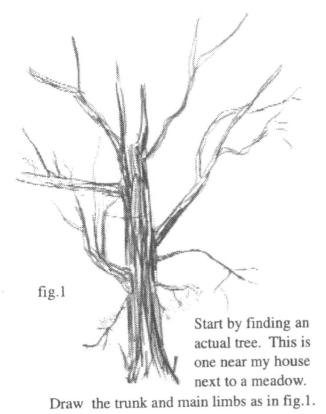

fig.1

Start by finding an actual tree. This is one near my house next to a meadow.

Draw the trunk and main limbs as in fig.1.

fig.3

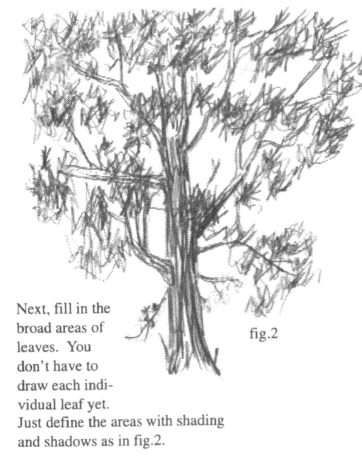

Next, fill in the broad areas of leaves. You don't have to draw each individual leaf yet.

Just define the areas with shading and shadows as in fig.2.

fig.2

Now draw individual leaves. Using light and dark leaves to intensify the shadows, give depth to the shading and add highlights. Draw individual leaves apart from the shadows or groups of leaves. These individual leaves can be "not connected" to anything, or you may want to draw fine lines to them to indicate the small twigs. Lastly, draw the ground line.

My backyard in mid-summer when my mower is broken.

Drawing rocks, trees, and other natural objects are as easy as anything else. Define the space, shape add shadow and shade and then texture. Also, just like everything else, draw what you see not what you think you see.

If you cannot go outside, or if what you see outside isn't interesting enough for you, find a wonderful landscape that is a photograph, and modify it to be your own. Remember that in a landscape things in the foreground are darker and clearer; and as you go farther away they recede into the color of the distance, be it mountain or sky or sea. Look the following landscapes and notice how these observation hold true. Use a photograph of a landscape, but do not copy it exactly. Make changes and improve and rearrange different areas of it. Because you are changing and rearranging, darkening and lightening, you are also designing and composing your own composition.

When you draw from photos, you will need to do what I call an artist interpretation. You can never come up with the variety of colors seen in the nat-ural world. Some say they can identify more than 16.8 million colors mathematically. If you use every colour you have in your limited palette even with complete mixing, it is impossible to get to the range of colour in the real world. You have to enhance and interpret the picture to make it look right. If you try to make it look just like the photograph, it will look flat. With a photograph, your eye puts the picture together, knowing trees are round and walls are flat. In your picture you have to modify the surfaces of trees, rocks, vegetation and everything else by enhancing the shadows and shades and highlights in order for them to look real. When you are using black and white, because you cannot show roundness with color, you will need to use shading and shadow with your pencil to make something look round.

Generally speaking the more time you take, the more details you can see and incorporate into your pictures, the more realistic they will look.

I feel a little like Michaelangelo, when Pope Julius was trying to get him to hurry up and finish the Sistine Chapel. In the movie "The Agony an the Ecstacy" when Pope Julius would say, "When will you make an end?" Michaelangelo (Charleston Heston) would say, "When I'm finished." I feel like that now because I don't feel as if I have given you everything, besides I like to draw and I don't want to finish. I could do about three more lessons. They would be on drawing glass, cloth and cellophane. Each of those lessons would be repeating what I've already said. "Draw what you see, not what you think you see." I could add a few lines like, "Draw the shape first, look for dark areas by squinting your eyes at what you are drawing, and copy those dark areas to your work; then shading, shadow, and texture." On cellophane and glass, you draw the same as when you draw glasses on someone's face. Draw behind the glasses first, then the glasses. Drawing cloth is like everything else, shape, shadow and texture. There are always lots of things to practice drawing with cloth. People's clothes, table cloths, flags and window curtains, to name a few. Some good advice to you would be to tell you to go back and read the introduction and the first few pages of this book. I know you were in a hurry to get started drawing and probably skipped those first pages. There are some important things to know there, so look back at them. The rest of the good advice would be to continue to draw. **PRACTICE, PRACTICE, PRACTICE,** it cannot be said too much. You may want to go back through this book and do the lessons over. Start new sketches or look at the ones you did the first time through the book and redo them. Save the best pictures for your portfolio. If you ever go to art school or apply for a job as an artist they will want to see what you can do.

Finally, I believe that drawing is one of the most important skills you can learn. You can use this skill in other fields such as science and architecture. It can even come in handy in business. If you have an idea that you want to get across to someone who doesn't understand you might say,"Do you want me to draw you a picture?" I mention this because art is the universal language. It transcends all history and every culture. There has never been discovered any culture in all of history that did not have an art form. It is a universal language. All writings at one time were pictures, which changed over time into symbols. Now these symbols make up words contain meanings. Art in all of its forms carry meaning. The artist illustrates a message using many forms and not just drawing. But drawing is a basic underlying form that is necessary to do painting, watercolor or sculpture. Everyone should learn to draw. It helps develop their mind. But more importantly it is communication. It communicates what is within and without. How one views what is without is shaded by what a person has within. You are the hope of the world. You who have what is right within are the only ones who can correctly show what is right.

Matthew 6: 22* The light of the body is the eye: if therefore thine eye be single (pure), thy whole body shall be full of light.
 23 But if thine eye be evil, thy whole body shall be full of darkness. If therefore the light that is in thee be darkness, how great is that darkness!

When the world does art what could you expect? When you do art, now that should be different!

Enjoy drawing, enjoy art, have fun communicating truth to the world!
......

MORE BOOKS FROM VISUAL MANNA

Art Through the Core series...
  Teaching American History Through Art
  Teaching Astronomy Through Art
  Teaching English Through Art
  Teaching History Through Art
  Teaching Literature Through Art
  Teaching Math Through Art
  Teaching Science Through Art
  Teaching Social Studies Through Art

Other Books...
  Art Adventures in Narnia
  Art Basics for Children
  Bible Arts & Crafts
  Christian Holiday Arts & Crafts
  Dragons, Dinosaurs, Castles and Knights
  Drawing, Painting and Sculpting Horses
  Expanding Your Horizons Through Words
  Indians In Art
  Master Drawing
  Preschool & Early Elementary Art Basics
  Preschool Bible Lessons
  Visual Manna 1: Complete Art Curriculum
  Visual Manna 2: Advanced Techniques

Books available at Rainbow Resource Center:
www.rainbowresource.com • 888.841.3456

VISUAL|
|MANNA

Educating with art since 1992!

A Christian is one whose imagination should fly
beyond the stars. Francis Schaeffer

HIS LIONS

Contact *visualmanna@gmail.com* if you are interested in our Intern program. Students learn how to teach art, do murals for ministry, prepare an excellent portfolio, and much more. Go to **visualmanna.com** for information.

Free art lessons are available at **OurHomeschoolForum.com** and books are available at Rainbow Resource Center (**www.rainbowresource.com**). Try all our "Art Through the Core" series and other books as well! Make learning fun for kids!!! Sharon Jeffus teaches Art Intensives in person for the Landry Academy at **landryacademy.com**.

Made in the USA
Monee, IL
11 October 2020